Conserving ecosystems amid climate challenges

Conserving ecosystems amid climate challenges

Hurmuz Ain

UNIEK ENTERPRISES

CONTENTS

Introduction

1. Definition of Ecosystem Conservation
2. The Urgency of Climate Challenges
3. Purpose and Objectives of the Book

INTRODUCTION

The 21st century has introduced a time of exceptional natural difficulties, with environmental change remaining at the very front of worldwide worries. As our planet wrestles with increasing temperatures, outrageous climate occasions, and the deficiency of biodiversity, the basic to ration environments has become more basic than any time in recent memory. Environments, the mind boggling trap of interconnected organic networks and their actual surroundings, assume a basic part in supporting life on The planet. They offer fundamental types of assistance like clean air and water, fertilization of harvests, environment guideline, and natural surroundings for incalculable species. In any case, these biological systems are under extreme danger because of human-prompted environmental change, presenting huge dangers to both the climate and human prosperity.

Understanding the Nexus of Biological systems and Environmental Change:
To appreciate the earnestness of monitoring environments despite environment challenges, investigating the unpredictable nexus between these two elements is fundamental. Environmental change, principally determined by human exercises like consuming petroleum products and deforestation, has broad results on biological systems across the globe. One of the most obvious effects is the modification of temperature and precipitation designs, prompting shifts in the circulation of species and the planning of natural occasions, a peculiarity usually known as phenological changes.

Climbing worldwide temperatures have additionally sped up the softening of polar ice covers and ice sheets, adding to the ocean level ascent. This, thusly, compromises beach front biological systems and the networks subject to them. Also, outrageous climate occasions like tropical storms, dry spells, and rapidly spreading fires are turning out to be more incessant and extraordinary, making quick and long haul harm environments. These interruptions frequently lead to environment misfortune, discontinuity, and debasement, fueling the weakness of various species.

Biodiversity, the assortment of life on The planet, is complicatedly connected to the wellbeing and flexibility of biological systems. Environmental change represents a double danger to biodiversity by straightforwardly influencing species and by modifying the living spaces they rely upon. The Intergovernmental Board on Environmental Change (IPCC) reports that a warming environment represents a huge gamble to various species, particularly those with restricted capacity to adjust or move. As temperatures climb, a few animal types might find their current natural surroundings unfriendly, prompting populace declines or even termination.

Moderating biological systems isn't just urgent for safeguarding biodiversity yet in addition for alleviating the effects of environmental change. Solid biological systems go about as carbon sinks, sequestering a lot of carbon dioxide from the climate. Woodlands, specifically, assume a urgent part in carbon sequestration, assisting with controlling the World's environment. Notwithstanding, wild deforestation, frequently determined by rural extension and logging, has fundamentally diminished the limit of environments to ingest and store carbon.

The Financial Ramifications of Environment Corruption:

The debasement of biological systems because of environmental change conveys significant financial ramifications, especially for networks that are intently attached to regular assets for their livelihoods. Waterfront people group, for instance, face the double test of rising ocean levels and the deficiency of significant fisheries because of changes in sea temperature and causticity. Horticulture, one more area exceptionally subject to environment and biological system administrations, is powerless against shifts in precipitation designs, expanded recurrence of outrageous climate occasions, and the spread of vermin and sicknesses.

Moreover, the deficiency of biodiversity and biological system administrations can have flowing impacts on different ventures, including drugs, agribusiness, and the travel industry. Numerous drugs are gotten from plant and creature species tracked down in different biological systems, and the deficiency of these species could obstruct future revelations of restorative mixtures. Rural frameworks depend on pollinators, soil ripeness, and water guideline given by environments, and disturbances to these administrations can have serious ramifications for food creation. Additionally, environments, for example, coral reefs and rainforests draw in great many vacationers every year, and their corruption influences nearby economies as well as reduces the tasteful and social worth of these regular miracles.

Tending to Environment Difficulties through Biological system Preservation:

Perceiving the many-sided linkages among biological systems and environmental change, there is a developing agreement on the requirement for coordinated and all encompassing ways to deal with protection. Conventional preservation methodologies frequently centered around safeguarding individual species or safeguarded regions. While these endeavors stay significant, a change in outlook towards biological system based preservation is crucial for address the more extensive effects of environmental change.

Safeguarded Regions and Biodiversity Preservation:

Reinforcing and extending safeguarded regions: Vigorous safeguarded regions are fundamental for protecting biodiversity and giving environments to species to flourish. Legislatures and global associations should work cooperatively to lay out and keep up with all around oversaw safeguarded regions.

Environmental halls: Making natural passages that associate divided living spaces considers the development of species, advancing hereditary variety and upgrading the flexibility of biological systems despite environmental change.

Feasible Land The executives:

Keeping away from deforestation and advancing afforestation: Stopping deforestation and advancing afforestation endeavors are vital for keeping up with carbon sinks and protecting biodiversity. Feasible land the board rehearses, for example, agroforestry, can add to both environment relief and transformation.

Reforestation drives: Carrying out enormous scope reforestation drives can assist with reestablishing corrupted environments, upgrade carbon sequestration, and give numerous advantages to neighborhood networks.

Environment Versatile Farming:

Maintainable farming works on: Empowering the reception of supportable rural practices, for example, agroecology, can upgrade the versatility of horticultural frameworks to environmental change. These practices focus on soil wellbeing, water protection, and biodiversity preservation.

Expansion of yields: Advancing the enhancement of harvests can assist with moderating the dangers related with environmental change, including the spread of bugs and illnesses. Agro-biodiversity is urgent for keeping up with strong and useful farming frameworks.

Coordinated Water Asset The executives:

Safeguarding freshwater biological systems: Environments, for example, wetlands and watersheds assume a fundamental part in controlling water stream, quality, and accessibility. Securing and reestablishing these environments is fundamental for guaranteeing a maintainable and versatile water supply notwithstanding changing environment conditions.

Local area Commitment and Strengthening:

Including neighborhood networks: Drawing in nearby networks in preservation endeavors is central for progress. Native information and customary practices frequently hold important bits of knowledge for supportable environment the board, and cooperation with nearby networks guarantees the drawn out suitability of preservation drives.

Enabling people group through schooling: Instructing people group about the significance of environments, environmental change, and economical practices encourages a feeling of stewardship. Informed people group are bound to effectively partake in protection endeavors and promoter for strategy changes.

Global Coordinated effort and Strategy Structures:

Worldwide participation: Environmental change and biological system protection are worldwide difficulties that require facilitated global endeavors. Countries should team up to share assets, information, and advancements to resolve the interconnected issues of environmental change and biodiversity misfortune.

Reinforcing peaceful accords: Improving and upholding peaceful accords, for example, the Paris Arrangement and the Show on Natural Variety is pivotal for setting aggressive targets and guaranteeing responsibility in tending to environment and biodiversity challenges.

1. **Definition of Ecosystem Conservation**

   Environment preservation is a complete and complex methodology pointed toward protecting the complicated equilibrium of life on The planet. At its center, it includes the insurance, the board, and reclamation of environments to guarantee their versatility, usefulness, and maintainability. This preservation worldview perceives the innate relationship of living life forms and their surroundings, stressing the need to protect biodiversity, biological cycles, and the administrations environments give. As human exercises keep on applying exceptional tensions on the regular world, understanding and characterizing environment preservation turns out to be progressively crucial for the prosperity of the planet and its occupants.

   Characterizing Environment Protection:

   Safeguarding Biodiversity:

   Species Protection: At the core of environment protection lies the conservation of biodiversity - the assortment of life on The planet. This incorporates magnetic species as well as the aggregate of the organic range, from microorganisms to dominant hunters. Protection endeavors center around shielding imperiled species, forestalling the deficiency of hereditary variety, and keeping up with solid populace elements inside biological systems.

   Hereditary Variety: Environment protection perceives the significance of hereditary variety inside species. Hereditary varieties improve flexibility to ecological changes, guaranteeing the versatility of populaces. Preservation systems frequently include keeping up with suitable populaces that can endure difficulties like infection flare-ups, environment adjustments, or environment vacillations.

   Keeping up with Natural Cycles:

   Biological system Administrations: Environments give a horde of administrations that are irreplaceable to human prosperity. These incorporate yet are not restricted to clean air and water, fertilization of yields, guideline of environment, and the arrangement of food and medication. Preservation endeavors endeavor to safeguard the environmental cycles that support these administrations, perceiving their significant job in supporting life and supporting human social orders.

Carbon Sequestration: Environments, especially timberlands, go about as crucial carbon sinks, engrossing and putting away carbon dioxide from the air. This mitigates the effects of environmental change by controlling worldwide temperatures. Biological system preservation includes measures to forestall deforestation, advance afforestation, and reestablish corrupted scenes to upgrade carbon sequestration.

Living space Conservation and Rebuilding:

Safeguarded Regions: Laying out and keeping up with safeguarded regions is a foundation of environment preservation. These regions act as safe-havens for different verdure, giving undisturbed living spaces where regular cycles can unfurl. Shielded regions range from public parks and natural life stores to marine safe-havens, each intended to protect explicit environments and their occupants.

Living space Reclamation: notwithstanding security, environment protection frequently includes dynamic rebuilding endeavors. Debased living spaces, whether because of human exercises, environmental change, or cataclysmic events, can be restored to recover their natural usefulness. Rebuilding ventures might incorporate reforestation, wetland recovery, and coral reef reclamation.

Feasible Asset The board:

Adjusting Human Necessities and Preservation: Biological system protection perceives the significance of addressing human requirements while guaranteeing the manageability of normal assets. This includes taking on rehearses that consider the extraction of assets without compromising the drawn out wellbeing of environments. Economical ranger service, fisheries the executives, and capable farming are indispensable parts of this methodology.

Monetary Valuation of Environments: Doling out financial worth to biological systems and their administrations is a technique to underscore their significance in dynamic cycles. This valuation considers the unmistakable and immaterial advantages given by environments, empowering a more comprehensive and economical way to deal with asset the executives.

Environmental Change Variation and Moderation:

Improving Versatility: Environment preservation is inherently connected to environmental change variation. As worldwide temperatures increase and weather conditions shift, biological systems face remarkable difficulties. Protection procedures expect to upgrade the flexibility of environments, permitting them to adjust to changing circumstances and keep up with their natural capabilities.

Moderating Environmental Change: Solid biological systems assume an essential part in relieving environmental change by sequestering carbon, managing temperatures, and impacting weather conditions. Preservation endeavors add to worldwide environment relief objectives by safeguarding existing carbon sinks, reestablishing corrupted biological systems, and advancing reasonable land the board rehearses.

Local area Commitment and Backing:

Comprehensive Preservation: Perceiving the interconnectedness of environments with human social orders, biological system protection effectively includes neighborhood networks. Comprehensive preservation approaches regard native information, conventional practices, and the freedoms of nearby networks. Connecting with networks in dynamic cycles encourages a feeling of responsibility and stewardship, guaranteeing the drawn out progress of preservation drives.

Promotion and Instruction: Environment preservation stretches out past actual insurance and reclamation; it incorporates bringing issues to light and supporting for strategy changes. Instruction drives assist with building a more extensive comprehension of the significance of environments and biodiversity, motivating aggregate activity at neighborhood, public, and worldwide levels.

Challenges in Biological system Preservation:

While the meaning of biological system preservation envelops an expansive range of techniques and standards, various difficulties block its viable execution:

Fracture and Living space Misfortune:

Urbanization, horticulture, and framework improvement frequently lead to natural surroundings discontinuity and misfortune. This represents a huge danger to biological systems and their capacity to help different vegetation.

Obtrusive Species:

The presentation of non-local species can upset environments by outcompeting local species, spreading sicknesses, and adjusting biological cycles. Overseeing obtrusive species is a perplexing test in numerous protection endeavors.

Environmental Change Effects:

The quick speed of environmental change presents extraordinary difficulties to biological system protection. Climbing temperatures, outrageous climate occasions, and changes in precipitation examples can subvert the flexibility of biological systems and the species they support.

Overexploitation of Assets:

Unreasonable double-dealing of normal assets, whether through overfishing, deforestation, or extreme hunting, compromises the equilibrium of biological systems and lessens their capacity to offer fundamental types of assistance.

Absence of Financing and Assets:

Protection endeavors frequently face monetary requirements, restricting the degree and adequacy of drives. Sufficient financing and assets are vital for the effective execution of biological system protection projects.

Globalization and Exchange:

Worldwide exchange can work with the spread of sicknesses, intrusive species, and impractical asset extraction, presenting difficulties for limited preservation endeavors.

Strategy and Administration Holes:

Deficient strategies, frail requirement, and administration holes can subvert preservation endeavors. Reinforcing legitimate structures and worldwide participation is fundamental for tending to these difficulties.

2. **The Urgency of Climate Challenges**

Environmental change remains as one of the most squeezing and pressing difficulties within recent memory. The World's environment is going through remarkable movements, driven to a great extent by human exercises that discharge ozone harming substances into the climate. The results are extensive and influence environments, biodiversity, and the actual texture of human social orders. As the earnestness of environment challenges turns out to be progressively apparent, it is vital to dive into the complex parts of this worldwide emergency.

The Speeding up Speed of Environmental Change:

One of the central attributes of the ongoing environment challenge is the speeding up speed of progress. Worldwide temperatures are increasing at a disturbing rate, bringing about more successive and serious heatwaves, storms, and other outrageous climate occasions. The Intergovernmental Board on Environmental Change (IPCC) reports that human exercises have unequivocally warmed the planet, and pressing activity is expected to relieve further effects.

Influences on Biological systems and Biodiversity:

Environmental change represents a serious danger to biological systems all over the planet. Increasing temperatures, adjusted precipitation designs, and changing sea conditions disturb the fragile equilibrium of these frameworks. Coral reefs, rainforests, and polar environments are especially helpless, confronting uncommon pressure and debasement. The deficiency of biodiversity isn't just a biological misfortune yet in addition sabotages the versatility of environments to adjust to evolving conditions.

Rising Ocean Levels and Seaside Weakness:

One of the most substantial outcomes of environmental change is the ascent in ocean levels. As polar ice melts and glacial masses subside, waterfront regions face expanded dangers of immersion and disintegration. Low-lying island countries and thickly populated seaside urban communities are on the cutting edge, wrestling with the critical requirement for variation measures to safeguard networks and framework.

Social and Financial Consequences:

Environment challenges are not restricted to the normal world; they have significant social and monetary repercussions. Weak people group, frequently least liable for ozone depleting substance emanations, endure the worst part of environment influences. Expanded recurrence of outrageous climate occasions prompts dislodging, loss of occupations, and uplifted food weakness. The earnest requirement for flexibility building measures becomes apparent as social orders wrestle with the raising expenses of environment related calamities.

Worldwide Imbalance and Environment Equity:

The criticalness of environment challenges is exacerbated by worldwide imbalances. Created countries generally contributed fundamentally to fossil fuel byproducts, while non-industrial countries bear a lopsided weight of the effects. The idea of environment equity underscores the moral basic to address these differences, featuring the critical requirement for aggregate and impartial activity to relieve environmental change and help weak networks in adjusting to its belongings.

Input Circles and Tipping Focuses:

An especially unsettling part of environment direness is the presence of input circles and potential tipping focuses. Positive input circles, like the arrival of methane from dissolving permafrost, could intensify warming patterns. Tipping focuses address basic edges where moderately little changes could prompt sudden and irreversible outcomes, accentuating the earnestness to forestall flowing and wild effects.

The Job of Ozone harming substance Emanations:

Key to the earnestness of environment challenges is the tenacious expansion in ozone depleting substance emanations. Carbon dioxide, methane, and nitrous oxide levels have arrived at phenomenal highs, principally because of the consuming of petroleum products, deforestation, and modern cycles. The critical need to change to low-carbon and reasonable practices is central in relieving further environment destabilization.

Political Will and Global Participation:

Tending to environment challenges requires not just pressing activity at the individual and local area levels yet in addition an aggregate worldwide exertion. Peaceful accords, for example, the Paris Understanding, highlight the requirement for countries to team up in diminishing emanations and adjusting to environment influences. Be that as it may, the earnestness lies in changing responsibilities into substantial activities, with states, organizations, and common society cooperating to accomplish significant outcomes.

Innovation and Development as Objectives:

Saddling innovation and cultivating advancement are basic parts of tending to the desperation of environment challenges. Headways in environmentally friendly power, manageable agribusiness, and carbon catch advances offer promising roads for alleviating emanations and building environment flexibility.

Critical interests in innovative work can catalyze groundbreaking answers for explore the intricacies of the environment emergency.

Individual and Local area Activity:

While foundational changes are goal, individual and local area activities likewise assume a pivotal part. The earnestness of environment challenges requires far reaching mindfulness, instruction, and conduct shifts. Supportable practices, energy preservation, and capable utilization are fundamental parts of the aggregate work to relieve environmental change.

3. **Purpose and Objectives of the Book**

In the immense scene of writing, each book fills a need, and its targets guide the peruser through an excursion of investigation, edification, or change. "Exploring the Void" is no exemption, as it sets out on a nuanced investigation of significant subjects, winding around together stories that test, motivate, and incite reflection. This extensive conversation will dive into the reason and targets that shape the quintessence of the book, offering perusers a guide for the scholarly and close to home odyssey that lies ahead.

Reason: Revealing the Profundities of Human Experience

At the core of "Exploring the Void" lies an essential reason — to dig into the profundities of the human experience. The book looks to disentangle the intricacies of presence, welcoming perusers to explore the allegorical chasm of life's difficulties, vulnerabilities, and significant minutes. Through a rich embroidery of stories, viewpoints, and experiences, the book means to enlighten the shadows, empowering perusers to defy the obscure with interest and flexibility.

Investigation of Human Versatility:

The book endeavors to commend the strength intrinsic in the human soul. Through powerful stories and character ventures, it expects to exhibit the exceptional capacity of people to explore through affliction, track down strength in weakness, and arise changed on the opposite side.

Reflection on Existential Inquiries:

"Exploring the Chasm" welcomes perusers to draw in with existential inquiries that have fascinated mankind for quite a long time. By investigating subjects of direction, significance, mortality, and the quest for character, the book urges perusers to leave on an individual journey for understanding and self-disclosure.

Challenge to Regular Viewpoints:

A focal motivation behind the book is to challenge regular points of view and cultural standards. It attempts to disturb agreeable stories, provoking perusers to address suspicions, defy predispositions, and grow how they might interpret the assorted encounters that shape the human condition.

Impetus for Sympathy and Understanding:

Through different characters and accounts, the book plans to cultivate sympathy and understanding. By drenching perusers in the existences of others, it looks to separate boundaries, rise above contrasts, and make a space for discourse and association across different societies, foundations, and encounters.

Goals: Exploring the Scholarly Territory

The goals of "Exploring the Void" are complicatedly woven into the texture of the account. Every section, character, and topical investigation fills a particular need, adding to the general objectives of the book.

Complex Person Improvement:

An essential goal is to make complex and interesting characters that resound with perusers. By digging into the intricacies of their encounters, inspirations, and changes, the book means to offer a mirror to the peruser's own excursion and incite contemplation.

Interconnected Story Strings:

The book utilizes an interconnected story structure, winding around together dissimilar stories that combine and separate like streams meeting in a tremendous sea. This primary decision serves the target of representing the interconnectedness of human encounters, stressing that singular stories are important for a bigger, shared embroidery.

Investigation of Kind Adaptability:

"Exploring the Chasm" embraces sort adaptability as a goal. Moving flawlessly between sorts — from dramatization to dream, verifiable fiction to speculative fiction — the book means to enthrall assorted crowds while exhibiting the flexibility of narrating as a device for investigating various features of the human experience.

Scholarly Incitement:

Scholarly incitement is a foundation objective. The book attempts to invigorate decisive reasoning by introducing thoughts, situations, and moral issues that welcome perusers to consider their own convictions, values, and viewpoints.

Through this, it tries to be in excess of a uninvolved understanding encounter, developing into an impetus for smart talk.

Imaginative Language and Symbolism:

A target of "Exploring the Chasm" is to utilize imaginative language and distinctive symbolism. The exposition is created with an accentuation on suggestive depictions and melodious articulations, welcoming perusers to appreciate the story as well as submerge themselves in the tactile and profound scenes painted by the words.

Worldly and Spatial Investigation:

The book plans to rise above transient and spatial limits. By investigating different time spans, settings, and social settings, it looks to offer perusers an all encompassing perspective on the human experience. This goal adds to a rich embroidery that mirrors the variety and all inclusiveness of the difficulties and wins that characterize us.

The Peruser's Job: Dynamic Commitment and Translation

While the reason and goals lay the basis for "Exploring the Pit," the peruser's job is similarly urgent. The book energizes dynamic commitment, welcoming perusers to become co-makers of importance and translation.

Intelligent Story Components:

The consideration of intelligent story components is purposeful. Whether through unconditional plotlines, uncertain person inspirations, or elective endings, the book urges perusers to take part in forming the significance of the story effectively. This intuitive quality changes the demonstration of adding something extra to a dynamic and individual experience.

Conversation and Local area Building:

A key goal is to encourage conversation and local area building. The book gives conversation prompts, topical inquiries, and strengthening materials to urge perusers to participate in significant discussions with others. This mutual viewpoint adds to the more extensive objective of making a common space for reflection and investigation.

Advancement of Basic Education:

Basic education is a center goal. By introducing layered stories and nuanced characters, "Exploring the Pit" provokes perusers to address suspicions, dissect inspirations, and decipher imagery. This approach plans to develop decisive reasoning abilities that stretch out past the pages of the book.

Individual Reflection and Journaling:

The book empowers individual reflection and journaling. Coordinated prompts and spaces for individual notes all through the text welcome perusers to interface the story to their own lives, encouraging a more profound degree of thoughtfulness and self-revelation.

Chapter 1

Understanding Climate Change's Impact on Ecosystems

Environmental change, driven principally by human exercises like the consuming of petroleum derivatives and deforestation, has arisen as one of the most squeezing worldwide difficulties within recent memory. As the World's environment goes through critical modifications, biological systems all over the planet are encountering significant effects. These progressions are upsetting the fragile equilibrium of biodiversity, modifying biological systems' construction and capability, and presenting dangers to the incalculable species that rely upon stable natural circumstances. In this far reaching investigation, we will dive into the complex manners by which environmental change is influencing biological systems, analyzing the natural, social, and monetary outcomes of these changes.

1. **The Systems of Environmental Change**

   Prior to digging into the effect of environmental change on biological systems, it is vital to comprehend the components driving worldwide environmental change. The essential driver is the expansion in ozone depleting substance fixations in the World's environment. Human exercises, like the consuming of petroleum derivatives, deforestation, and modern cycles, discharge a lot of carbon dioxide (CO2), methane (CH4), and nitrous oxide (N2O) into the air. These gases trap heat, prompting the warming of the planet — a peculiarity normally alluded to as the nursery impact. The outcomes of this warming are far reaching and influence different parts of the World's environment framework. Changes in temperature designs, adjusted precipitation systems, and disturbances to normal environment fluctuation add to the overall effect of environmental change on biological systems.

2. **Increasing Temperatures and Modified Environment Examples**

One of the most immediate and perceptible impacts of environmental change is the climb in worldwide temperatures. This warming pattern has extensive ramifications for biological systems around the world. Temperature impacts organic cycles, from the development of plants to the way of behaving of creatures. As temperatures increment, biological systems are compelled to adjust to new warm circumstances, prompting shifts in species appropriation and changes in the planning of key natural occasions.

Hotter temperatures likewise add to the softening of polar ice covers and ice sheets, prompting rising ocean levels. This represents an immediate danger to waterfront environments, as saltwater interruption can adversely influence freshwater territories, and numerous species might battle to adjust to these changes. Also, the expanded recurrence and power of heatwaves can bring about heat pressure for different organic entities, prompting physiological and social changes.

Adjusted environment designs, remembering changes for precipitation and the recurrence of outrageous climate occasions, further fuel the difficulties looked by biological systems. Areas that once experienced unsurprising precipitation may now confront more successive and serious dry seasons, while others might see expanded precipitation and flooding. These progressions can disturb the fragile equilibrium of environments, influencing the accessibility of water assets, soil dampness levels, and the dispersion of plant and creature species.

3. **Sea Fermentation and Warming**

The world's seas assume a basic part in directing the World's environment, retaining huge amounts of intensity and carbon dioxide. Be that as it may, this ingestion includes some significant pitfalls. As the convergence of climatic CO2 builds, the seas become more acidic — a peculiarity known as sea fermentation. This has significant ramifications for marine biological systems, especially those that depend on calcium carbonate, like coral reefs and shelled living beings.

Sea fermentation can prompt the crumbling of coral reefs, which are among the most different and financially significant environments in the world. Coral fading, a peculiarity where corals oust their harmonious green growth in light of pressure, is turning out to be more normal as ocean temperatures climb. This undermines the endurance of coral reefs as well as effects the bunch species that rely upon these biological systems for safe house and food.

Notwithstanding fermentation, the warming of sea waters adds to changes in marine environments. Numerous types of fish, for instance, are exceptionally delicate to temperature varieties. As waters warm, some fish might relocate to cooler areas, influencing the jobs of networks that rely upon fisheries. The changed dissemination of marine species can likewise upset food networks, prompting flowing impacts all through the whole environment.

4. **Influences on Earthbound Biological systems**

Environmental change has expansive ramifications for earthbound biological systems, enveloping woods, fields, deserts, and that's just the beginning. Changes in temperature and precipitation designs impact the development and appropriation of plant species, which, thus, influence the creatures that rely upon them for food and territory.

Changes in Vegetation and Biome Circulation

As temperatures climb, plant species might move to higher scopes or rises looking for additional reasonable climatic circumstances. This can bring about shifts in vegetation examples and changes to the sythesis of plant networks. Now and again, whole biomes might be adjusted, with significant ramifications for the species that occupy these regions.

For example, in boreal woodlands, where the predominant tree species are adjusted to cold environments, warming temperatures might prompt the toward the north movement of these timberlands. This can influence the species that are interestingly adjusted to these environments, as well as the native networks that depend on them for their conventional vocations.

Expanded Recurrence of Out of control fires

The blend of higher temperatures, delayed dry seasons, and changes in vegetation designs has added to an expanded recurrence and power of rapidly spreading fires in many regions of the planet. Fierce blazes assume a characteristic part in certain biological systems, advancing supplement cycling and molding vegetation elements. Be that as it may, the latest thing of additional regular and extreme out of control fires represents a critical danger to biodiversity and biological system security.

In environments where fire is definitely not a characteristic piece of the natural cycle, for example, specific kinds of backwoods, the effect can especially demolish. Enormous scope out of control fires can prompt the deficiency of territory for some species, including those that are as of now confronting dangers from other human exercises like natural surroundings annihilation and fracture.

Influence on Cold Environments

The Cold district is encountering probably the most quick changes because of environmental change. As temperatures in the Cold ascent at almost two times the worldwide normal, the effects on Icy biological systems are significant and colossal.

The liquefying of ocean ice not just influences polar bears and other ice-subordinate species yet in addition impacts the conveyance and overflow of marine life. For instance, the diminished degree of ocean ice modifies the accessibility of environment for seals, which are a urgent food hotspot for polar bears. This makes a cascading type of influence, affecting the whole Cold marine food web.

Ashore, defrosting permafrost represents extra difficulties. Permafrost contains a lot of natural carbon that has been saved in a frozen state for millennia. As permafrost defrosts, this carbon is delivered into the air as methane and carbon dioxide, adding to additional warming — a criticism circle that strengthens environmental change. Defrosting permafrost additionally prompts changes in the scene, influencing the territories of species adjusted to chilly, stable circumstances.

5. **Biodiversity Misfortune and Biological system Administrations**

Maybe one of the most huge and direct results of environmental change on biological systems is the deficiency of biodiversity. As the environment changes, numerous species wind up in conditions that never again suit their biological prerequisites. A few animal groups might have the option to adjust or move to additional reasonable environments, yet others might confront elimination.

Dangers to Jeopardized Species

Species that are now in danger because of elements like environment misfortune, contamination, and overexploitation are especially defenseless against the extra stressors forced by environmental change. For instance, certain famous species like the polar bear and the snow panther are confronting expanded dangers to their endurance because of the deficiency of their particular territories.

Creatures of land and water, known for their aversion to ecological changes, are additionally in danger. Environment actuated shifts in temperature and precipitation examples can affect the accessibility of appropriate rearing territories for the vast majority land and water proficient species. Also, the spread of illnesses worked with by changes in environment can additionally add to decreases in land and water proficient populaces.

Interruption of Biological system Administrations

Environments give a great many administrations that are fundamental for human prosperity. These biological system administrations incorporate the arrangement of clean water, guideline of environment, fertilization of yields, and the upkeep of soil richness. Environmental change represents a danger to the dependability and unwavering quality of these administrations.

For instance, changes in precipitation examples can influence water accessibility, prompting dry spells in certain districts and floods in others. This fluctuation can have serious ramifications for farming, influencing crop yields and food security. Also, the disturbance of fertilization administrations because of changes in the planning of blossoming and the circulation of pollinators can affect the creation of natural products, vegetables, and different harvests.

The deficiency of biodiversity additionally decreases the strength of biological systems to ecological stressors. Different biological systems are better ready to adjust to changes and recuperate from aggravations, like outrageous climate occasions. As species vanish, the capacity of biological systems to offer types of assistance to people becomes compromised.

6. **Social and Monetary Ramifications**

The effects of environmental change on biological systems reach out past the domain of nature, influencing human social orders and economies. Weak people group, frequently those with restricted assets and versatile limit, face uplifted gambles from the progressions in biological systems achieved by environmental change.

Dangers to Vocations

Numerous people group all over the planet rely straightforwardly upon normal assets for their jobs, including agribusiness, fisheries, and ranger service. Changes in temperature, precipitation, and the recurrence of outrageous occasions can upset these exercises, presenting dangers to the financial prosperity of networks. For instance, networks that depend on means farming might confront decreased crop yields because of modified developing circumstances. Anglers might encounter decreases in fish populaces as marine biological systems go through changes. Native people group with profound associations with explicit biological systems might see the disintegration of their social practices and conventional information as these conditions change.

Expanded Environment Initiated Movement

As environmental change disturbs biological systems and undermines livelihoods, it can likewise add to constrained relocation. Networks that depend on horticulture might find it progressively hard to support their lifestyle because of changing environment conditions. Now and again, whole networks might be confronted with the possibility of movement as ocean levels rise or outrageous climate occasions make their flow areas appalling.

Environment incited relocation presents huge difficulties, for the networks straightforwardly impacted as well as for the locales getting uprooted populaces. This can prompt social pressures, burden on assets, and the potential for clashes over land and water.

Financial Expenses of Environment Interruption

The monetary expenses of environmental change-instigated disturbances to biological systems are significant. The deficiency of biological system administrations, for example, decreases in crop yields, expanded recurrence of catastrophic events, and the corruption of fisheries, can have flowing consequences for public economies.

States and organizations might confront inflated costs connected with adjusting to these progressions and alleviating their effects. Interests in framework to safeguard against flooding, measures to upgrade water security, and endeavors to progress to additional supportable rural practices are only a couple of instances of the financial reactions expected to address the outcomes of environmental change on biological systems.

7. **Moderation and Transformation Techniques**

Tending to the effects of environmental change on biological systems requires a blend of relief and variation methodologies. Relief means to diminish or forestall the discharge of ozone harming substances, accordingly restricting the degree of environmental change. Transformation includes acclimating to the progressions that are now happening, making biological systems stronger and assisting networks with adapting to the difficulties presented by an evolving environment.

Relief Techniques

Diminishing ozone harming substance discharges is basic to relieving the effects of environmental change on biological systems. This includes progressing to environmentally friendly power sources, further developing energy productivity, and carrying out approaches and practices that advance economical land use and ranger service.

Afforestation and reforestation drives can assume a urgent part in sequestering carbon and improving biodiversity. Backwoods go about as carbon sinks, catching and putting away a lot of carbon dioxide. Safeguarding existing backwoods and reestablishing corrupted ones add to both environmental change moderation and the protection of essential biological systems.

Worldwide participation is fundamental for powerful relief, as environmental change is a worldwide test that requires composed endeavors. Arrangements, for example, the Paris Understanding intend to unite nations to set focuses for discharge decrease and advance maintainable turn of events.

Variation Methodologies

Transformation methodologies center around building the flexibility of biological systems and networks to the progressions that are as of now in progress. This includes executing measures to safeguard weak territories, improving the versatile limit of species, and creating techniques to adapt to the social and monetary effects of environmental change.

In waterfront regions, for instance, variation measures might incorporate the rebuilding of normal obstructions, for example, mangroves and hills to safeguard against ocean level ascent and tempest floods. In horticultural frameworks, practices like harvest broadening, further developed water the board, and the improvement of environment strong assortments can upgrade the limit of networks to adapt to evolving conditions.

Environment based variation, which includes the protection and maintainable administration of biological systems to give advantages to the two individuals and biodiversity, is earning respect as a savvy and economical methodology. This approach perceives the interconnectedness of biological systems and their capacity to give numerous advantages, including environment strength.

8. **The Job of Worldwide Collaboration**

Given the worldwide idea of environmental change, global collaboration is critical for really tending to its effects on biological systems. Cooperative endeavors are expected to share information, innovation, and assets to help both moderation and transformation techniques.

Financing and Backing for Agricultural Countries

Emerging countries frequently bear a lopsided weight of the effects of environmental change, regardless of offering less to the emanation of ozone harming substances. Worldwide help is fundamental for assist these countries with building strength, adjust to evolving conditions, and progress to maintainable improvement pathways.

Monetary systems, for example, the Green Environment Asset, expect to activate assets to help emerging nations in their endeavors to address environmental change. Innovation move and limit building drives likewise assume a fundamental part in engaging countries to execute powerful techniques for biological system safeguarding and environment strength.

Logical Exploration and Checking

Continuous logical examination and observing are crucial to understanding the advancing effects of environmental change on biological systems. This information is fundamental for creating proof based arrangements and systems to alleviate and adjust to these changes.

Worldwide cooperation in logical undertakings, for example, the Intergovernmental Board on Environmental Change (IPCC), works with the amalgamation of worldwide logical information on environmental change. This data, thus, illuminates policymakers, assisting them with pursuing informed choices to safeguard environments and upgrade worldwide flexibility.

1.1 Overview of Climate Change Effects

Environmental change, driven by human exercises like the consuming of petroleum products and deforestation, is causing inescapable and extensive consequences for the planet's biological systems, weather conditions, and human social orders. The results of environmental change are fluctuated and perplexing, influencing all that from climbing worldwide temperatures to shifts in precipitation designs, ocean level ascent, and outrageous climate occasions. In this complete outline, we will investigate the vital impacts of environmental change across various spaces, stressing the desperation of tending to this worldwide test.

1. **Climbing Worldwide Temperatures**

   One of the most obvious and generally noticed effects of environmental change is the climb in worldwide temperatures. Over the course of the last 100 years, the World's typical temperature has expanded, with the most recent couple of many years being the hottest on record. This warming pattern is essentially credited to the expansion in ozone depleting substance fixations in the environment, catching intensity and prompting the nursery impact.

   The outcomes of climbing temperatures are different and influence different parts of the World's frameworks. One striking impact is the liquefying of glacial masses and ice covers, adding to rising ocean levels. As ice keeps on softening, especially in polar districts, it represents a danger to biological systems as well as effects beach front networks and low-lying regions.

   In addition, higher temperatures lead to changes in the dispersion of plant and creature species. Species that were once restricted to explicit scopes or rises might relocate to cooler locales, upsetting laid out environments and possibly prompting the deficiency of biodiversity. The planning of organic occasions, like blooming and relocation, is additionally impacted by temperature changes, influencing the fragile equilibrium of environments.

2. **Changes in Precipitation Examples**

   Environmental change is modifying worldwide precipitation designs, prompting shifts in the appropriation and force of precipitation and snowfall. A few districts might encounter more regular and extreme precipitation, prompting flooding and avalanches, while others might confront delayed dry seasons and water shortage.

   Outrageous climate occasions, like storms, twisters, and hurricanes, are turning out to be more extraordinary and regular because of the warming of the seas. These occasions achieve decimating influences on seaside regions, causing storm floods, flooding, and foundation harm. Changes in precipitation designs likewise influence freshwater assets, impacting the accessibility of water for farming, drinking, and modern purposes.

In districts where precipitation is diminishing, biological systems might confront difficulties connected with water shortage. This can prompt the corruption of environments, loss of biodiversity, and expanded rivalry for restricted water assets among various areas, including agribusiness and metropolitan regions.

3. **Ocean Level Ascent**

The dissolving of icy masses and ice covers, alongside the warm extension of seawater as it warms, adds to the ocean level ascent — an immediate outcome of environmental change. Rising ocean levels present huge dangers to beach front environments, framework, and networks.

Low-lying beach front regions and islands are especially powerless against ocean level ascent, confronting the gamble of immersion and saltwater interruption. Seaside biological systems, for example, mangroves and salt bogs, which act as vital territories and give insurance against storm floods, are under danger. The deficiency of these environments influences biodiversity as well as reduces the normal guards that beach front regions have against outrageous climate occasions.

Notwithstanding actual effects, ocean level ascent can prompt the relocation of networks as they are compelled to move inland. This presents difficulties connected with social, financial, and social disturbances, underscoring the interconnectedness of environmental change impacts across various areas.

4. **Sea Fermentation**

The ingestion of overabundance carbon dioxide (CO_2) by the world's seas is prompting a peculiarity known as sea fermentation. As the seas retain more CO_2, they become more acidic, representing a serious danger to marine life, particularly creatures that depend on calcium carbonate to construct their shells and skeletons.

Marine species like corals, mollusks, and specific sorts of microscopic fish are especially powerless against sea fermentation. For instance, coral reefs, frequently alluded to as the "rainforests of the ocean" because of their inconceivable biodiversity, face dying and debasement as the sharpness of the sea increments. The effects overflow through the marine food web, influencing fish populaces and the vocations of networks reliant upon fisheries.

The mix of sea fermentation and warming waters heightens the weight on marine environments, making difficulties for variation and flexibility. Alleviating the impacts of sea fermentation requires complete endeavors to lessen CO2 outflows and safeguard weak marine environments.

5. **Outrageous Climate Occasions**

Environmental change is related with an expansion in the recurrence and force of outrageous climate occasions. These occasions incorporate heatwaves, dry spells, tropical storms, floods, and fierce blazes. While outrageous climate occasions have consistently happened, the changing environment compounds their effects and can make them more erratic.

Heatwaves are turning out to be more continuous and extreme, with suggestions for human wellbeing, horticulture, and environments. Delayed times of outrageous intensity can prompt intensity stress in both human and creature populaces, influencing efficiency and expanding the gamble of intensity related ailments. Dry seasons, heightened by changing precipitation designs and higher temperatures, have far reaching ramifications for water accessibility, agribusiness, and environments.

Water shortage can prompt yield disappointments, food deficiencies, and clashes over restricted assets. In environments, delayed dry seasons can add to the debasement of territories, loss of biodiversity, and expanded weakness to out of control fires.

Tropical storms, twisters, and hurricanes are portrayed by more grounded breezes and heavier precipitation because of warming sea temperatures. These tempests achieve horrendous tempest floods, flooding, and framework harm, especially in seaside regions. The rising power of these occasions presents difficulties for calamity readiness, reaction, and recuperation.

6. **Influence on Biodiversity**

Environmental change represents a huge danger to worldwide biodiversity, influencing species and biological systems across the planet. The interconnected idea of environments implies that adjustments of one region can have flowing impacts on the whole trap of life.

Species Terminations and Dissemination Movements

As temperatures climb and natural surroundings change, numerous species might end up in conditions that never again support their endurance. A few animal types might adjust by moving their reaches, while others might confront elimination. Environmental change goes about as an extra stressor on top of existing dangers, like living space misfortune, contamination, and over-exploitation.

Polar bears, for instance, are exceptionally subject to the ocean ice for hunting and are confronting difficulties as the ice dissolves. Essentially, species adjusted to explicit temperature and precipitation conditions might battle to get by in changed conditions. The disturbance of these species can significantly affect environments and the administrations they give to humankind.

Changes in Environment Construction

The creation and construction of environments are being adjusted by environmental change. Changes in temperature, precipitation, and the accessibility of water can influence the overflow and dispersion of plant species. This, thusly, impacts the herbivores and hunters that rely upon these plants.

At times, environments might go through movements to altogether new states, prompting the deficiency of recognizable scenes and territories. For example, as boreal woodlands move toward the north in light of warming temperatures, the species that once occupied these regions might confront provokes in adjusting to the evolving conditions.

Interruption of Natural Connections

Environmental change can upset the many-sided connections between species inside biological systems. For instance, the planning of key occasions in the existence pattern of various species, like blossoming, fertilization, and relocation, may become skewed because of changing natural circumstances. This can prompt a breakdown in natural communications and conditions.

Pollinators, like honey bees and butterflies, depend on unambiguous blooming times to correspond with their regenerative cycles. Changes in temperature and precipitation examples can disturb this synchronization, affecting the two plants and pollinators. Likewise, hunters and prey might encounter shifts in their dissemination, affecting the elements of food networks.

7. **Social and Financial Effects**

The impacts of environmental change are not bound to the regular world; they have significant ramifications for human social orders and economies. Weak people group, frequently those with restricted assets and versatile limit, are lopsidedly impacted by the effects of environmental change.

Dangers to Food Security

Changes in temperature and precipitation designs straightforwardly influence agribusiness, influencing crop yields and food creation. Changes in the accessibility of water, expanded recurrence of outrageous climate occasions, and the spread of bugs and sicknesses add to the difficulties looked by ranchers.

In certain locales, changing environment conditions might open up new open doors for farming, while in others, it might prompt diminished efficiency and expanded weakness. Also, the deficiency of biodiversity and interruptions to environments can influence the accessibility of wild food sources, further undermining food security for weak populaces.

Water Shortage and Rivalry

Changes in precipitation designs and expanded dissipation because of higher temperatures add to water shortage in numerous areas. This has suggestions for both agribusiness and human utilization. Contest for restricted water assets can prompt contentions, especially in regions where water is now a scant item.

Rustic people group subject to agribusiness might confront difficulties in getting adequate water for water system, affecting harvest yields and occupations. Metropolitan regions, as well, may battle to satisfy the needs of developing populaces as water accessibility turns out to be more dubious.

Wellbeing Dangers

Environmental change presents dangers to human wellbeing through different pathways. Heatwaves, exacerbated by increasing temperatures, can prompt intensity related ailments and passings. Changes in the appropriation of illness vectors, for example, mosquitoes conveying jungle fever or ticks sending Lyme sickness, acquaint new wellbeing gambles with populaces.

Outrageous climate occasions, including tropical storms, floods, and fierce blazes, can cause wounds, relocation, and the breakdown of medical services framework. Moreover, the mental cost of living in regions over and over impacted by environment related fiascos adds to emotional wellness challenges.

Dislodging and Relocation

As environmental change influences become more serious, weak networks might confront the possibility of uprooting. Rising ocean levels, outrageous climate occasions, and changes in rural efficiency can compel individuals to move looking for more secure and more reasonable day to day environments.

Environment incited relocation presents difficulties for the networks straightforwardly impacted as well as for the districts getting dislodged populaces. This can prompt social pressures, burden on assets, and possible struggles over land and water.

Monetary Expenses

The monetary expenses of environmental change are significant, influencing both created and emerging countries. The harms brought about by outrageous climate occasions, loss of horticultural efficiency, and the effects on foundation add to critical monetary misfortunes.

State run administrations and organizations should put resources into variation measures, like structure versatile framework and creating environment strong horticultural practices. Moreover, the expenses related with medical services, catastrophe reaction, and restoration further strain public spending plans.

8. Moderation and Variation Procedures

Tending to the effects of environmental change requires a double methodology including both relief and variation techniques. Alleviation expects to decrease or forestall the outflow of ozone depleting substances, while transformation centers around building strength to the progressions that are now in progress.

Moderation Procedures

Moderating environmental change requires diminishing the outflow of ozone harming substances, principally carbon dioxide (CO_2), methane (CH_4), and nitrous oxide (N_2O). Key relief techniques include:

1. **Change to Environmentally friendly power:** Moving from petroleum derivatives to environmentally friendly power sources, for example, sunlight based, wind, and hydropower, is pivotal for diminishing fossil fuel byproducts from energy creation.

2. **Energy Effectiveness:** Further developing energy proficiency in businesses, transportation, and structures helps decline in general energy utilization and outflows.

3. **Reforestation and Afforestation:** Safeguarding existing timberlands and establishing new trees assist with sequestering carbon dioxide, going about as carbon sinks.

4. **Economical Farming:** Carrying out manageable agrarian practices, for example, agroforestry and protection horticulture, can decrease emanations and upgrade carbon sequestration.

5. **Worldwide Participation:** Worldwide cooperation is fundamental for compelling relief, as environmental change is a common test that requires composed endeavors. Arrangements like the Paris Understanding set focuses for discharge decrease and advance global collaboration.

Variation Methodologies

Variation methodologies mean to improve the strength of biological systems and networks to the effects of environmental change. Key transformation systems include:

1. **Biological system Based Transformation:** Preserving and economically overseeing environments, like timberlands, wetlands, and waterfront regions, can improve versatility and give different advantages to the two individuals and biodiversity.

2. **Environment Strong Framework:** Planning and building foundation that can endure the effects of outrageous climate occasions, like floods and tropical storms, is pivotal for safeguarding networks.

3. **Water The executives:** Carrying out viable water the board works on, including water preservation, watershed insurance, and the improvement of strong water foundation, assists address with watering shortage challenges.

4. **Feasible Farming:** Taking on environment tough rural practices, like yield expansion, water-proficient water system, and the utilization of dry spell safe harvest assortments, upholds food security.

5. **Early Admonition Frameworks:** Creating and carrying out early advance notice frameworks for outrageous climate occasions helps networks get ready and clear ahead of time, diminishing the endangers of death toll and property.

IX. The Job of Global Collaboration

Given the transboundary idea of environmental change, global collaboration is principal for tending to its effects really. Cooperative endeavors are expected to share information, innovation, and assets to help both moderation and transformation methodologies.

Funding and Backing for Agricultural Countries

Emerging countries, frequently the most helpless against environmental change influences, need monetary and innovative help to execute powerful transformation measures. Drives, for example, the Green Environment Asset expect to assemble assets to help non-industrial nations in their endeavors to address environmental change.

Logical Exploration and Checking

Continuous logical exploration and observing are basic for understanding the developing effects of environmental change. Worldwide coordinated effort in logical undertakings, for example, the work directed by the Intergovernmental Board on Environmental Change (IPCC), works with the amalgamation of worldwide logical information. This data illuminates policymakers, assisting them with settling on proof based choices to safeguard environments and improve worldwide flexibility.

1.2 Vulnerability of Different Ecosystems

Biological systems overall fluctuate in their weakness to the effects of environmental change, featuring the different and unpredictable nature of Earth's natural embroidery. Icy and snow capped biological systems, described by chilly temperatures and specific greenery, are especially defenseless against increasing temperatures. The fast dissolving of permafrost in the Icy not just imperils the natural surroundings of famous species like polar bears yet in addition discharges put away carbon, adding to a criticism circle that heightens an Earth-wide temperature boost.

Waterfront biological systems, including mangroves, salt swamps, and coral reefs, face elevated weakness because of ocean level ascent and sea fermentation. These essential living spaces give favorable places to marine life, shield shores from storm floods, and backing different biological systems. The deficiency of these environments undermines biodiversity as well as jeopardizes the jobs of millions of individuals who rely upon waterfront assets.

Earthly environments, like tropical rainforests and boreal timberlands, stand up to difficulties connected with changing precipitation examples, out of control fires, and moving plant and creature disseminations. The interconnectedness of biological systems highlights the requirement for extensive preservation and versatile measures to relieve the weakness of various environments despite continuous environmental change.

1.3 Interconnectedness of Climate and Biodiversity

The connection among environment and biodiversity is profoundly interlaced, framing the foundation of Earth's biological equilibrium. Environment impacts the circulation, conduct, and life patterns of innumerable species, molding biological systems. On the other hand, biodiversity manages environment designs through processes like carbon sequestration and oxygen creation. In any case, human-prompted environmental change represents a huge danger, modifying territories, setting off eliminations, and upsetting complicated biological connections. Protecting biodiversity becomes an issue of natural preservation as well as a pivotal part in moderating environmental change influences, underscoring the mind boggling and harmonious connection between the soundness of the planet's biological systems and the solidness of its environment.

2

Chapter 2

Biodiversity Loss And Ecosystem Services

Biodiversity, the assortment of life on The planet, is basic to the wellbeing and working of environments. From tiny organic entities to magnetic megafauna, each specie assumes a part in keeping up with the sensitive equilibrium of nature. In any case, human exercises, especially those adding to environmental change, living space obliteration, contamination, and overexploitation, are speeding up the deficiency of biodiversity at an uncommon rate. As biodiversity declines, environments lose their versatility, and the administrations they give to mankind become compromised. In this investigation, we will dig into the complicated connection between biodiversity misfortune and environment administrations, looking at the broad ramifications for both the regular world and human social orders.

1. **The Significance of Biodiversity**

   Biodiversity is frequently alluded to as the "web of life" since it envelops the range of living creatures and the biological systems they occupy. This variety isn't simply a wellspring of stylish magnificence; the groundwork of various biological cycles support life on The planet. Biodiversity adds to environment strength, versatility, and flexibility, guaranteeing that biological systems can endure unsettling influences and keep on working over the long run.

Hereditary Variety

Hereditary variety inside species is pivotal for variation to changing ecological circumstances. It gives the natural substance to advancement, permitting species to foster characteristics that upgrade their capacity to get by and recreate. This is especially huge notwithstanding ecological stressors, for example, environmental change, where species with more noteworthy hereditary variety are bound to persevere and adjust.

Species Variety

Species variety, the wide range of creatures inside a biological system, advances environmental equilibrium. Every species possesses an extraordinary specialty, assuming a particular part in supplement cycling, fertilization, bug control, and other environmental cycles.

The passing of a solitary animal groups can upset these unpredictable connections, prompting flowing impacts all through the biological system.

Biological system Variety

Biological system variety alludes to the range of environments present on The planet, from tropical rainforests to icy tundras. Various environments offer extraordinary types of assistance and add to worldwide cycles, for example, the water cycle, carbon sequestration, and environment guideline. The deficiency of explicit biological systems reduces the general limit of the planet to support life and control natural circumstances.

2. **Environment Administrations**

Environment administrations are the advantages that people get from biological systems. These administrations can be classified into four fundamental sorts: provisioning administrations, managing administrations, social administrations, and supporting administrations. Every one of these administrations is complicatedly connected to the wellbeing and working of biological systems and, likewise, to the biodiversity inside them.

Provisioning Administrations

Provisioning administrations incorporate the unmistakable items that biological systems accommodate human utilization. These reach from food and wood to therapeutic plants and freshwater. Biodiversity assumes a basic part in guaranteeing the accessibility and variety of these assets. For instance, various plant species add to a large number of harvests, guaranteeing versatility even with irritations, illnesses, and changing natural circumstances.

Controlling Administrations

Managing administrations include the control of normal cycles that straightforwardly influence human prosperity. Biodiversity adds to the guideline of environment, water sanitization, fertilization of harvests, and the control of nuisances and illnesses. Woods, for example, go about as carbon sinks, assisting with moderating environmental change, while wetlands assume a urgent part in water filtration and flood control.

Social Administrations

Social administrations incorporate the non-material advantages that biological systems give, like sporting and tasteful qualities, otherworldly and social importance, and amazing open doors for instruction and examination. Biodiversity adds to the rich woven artwork of scenes and environments that individuals an incentive for their social and sporting encounters. Public parks, for example, are repositories of biodiversity as well as spaces for reflection and association with nature.

Supporting Administrations

Supporting administrations are the fundamental cycles that keep up with the circumstances essential for life on The planet. These incorporate supplement cycling, soil arrangement, and the support of biodiversity itself. Biodiversity is both a result of these supporting administrations and a fundamental part in their worked. The deficiency of biodiversity can upset these basic cycles, compromising the steadiness and versatility of biological systems.

3. **Dangers to Biodiversity**

In spite of the basic significance of biodiversity, human exercises have prompted a stunning loss of animal types and biological systems. A few key drivers add to this downfall:

Natural surroundings Obliteration and Discontinuity

The transformation of normal environments into rural land, metropolitan regions, and framework projects is a significant driver of biodiversity misfortune. Discontinuity of living spaces disengages populaces, making it moving for species to track down mates, food, and appropriate conditions. This discontinuity lessens hereditary variety and expands the weakness of species to elimination.

Environmental Change

Human-initiated environmental change is adjusting temperature and precipitation designs, affecting biological systems around the world. Species that can't adjust or relocate in light of these progressions face an expanded gamble of elimination. The warming of seas, sea fermentation, and the softening of polar ice further compromise marine biodiversity.

Overexploitation

The overharvesting of species for food, medication, pets, and different purposes has prompted populace declines and, at times, elimination. Overfishing, unlawful natural life exchange, and the unreasonable extraction of assets add to the consumption of biodiversity and upset environment elements.

Contamination

Contamination from agrarian spillover, modern release, and compound impurities adversely influences biodiversity. Pesticides, composts, and toxins modify soil and water quality, affecting the soundness of both earthbound and sea-going biological systems. Contamination additionally presents dangers to species through bioaccumulation, where poisons collect in creatures at higher trophic levels.

Obtrusive Species

The acquaintance of non-local species with new conditions, either purposefully or inadvertently, can inconveniently affect neighborhood biodiversity. Intrusive species can outcompete local species for assets, present new infections, and disturb laid out biological connections. This can prompt decreases in local populaces and the deficiency of biodiversity.

4. **Biodiversity Misfortune and Biological system Administration Decline**

The deficiency of biodiversity has immediate and significant ramifications for the administrations that biological systems give to humankind. Understanding these associations is significant for perceiving the worth of biodiversity past its characteristic worth and for planning techniques to address the continuous emergency.

Influence on Provisioning Administrations

The deficiency of biodiversity presents huge dangers to provisioning administrations, influencing the accessibility and variety of fundamental assets. In farming, where many harvests depend on fertilization, the decay of pollinators, for example, honey bees and butterflies risks crop yields and food security. Essentially, the deficiency of hereditary variety in plant and creature species decreases the strength of agrarian frameworks, making them more helpless to vermin, sicknesses, and changing ecological circumstances.

n fisheries, overexploitation and environment debasement lead to decreases in fish populaces, compromising the jobs of networks reliant upon fisheries. Amphibian biological systems, currently focused by contamination and environmental change, face further difficulties in giving supportable fish stocks.

Influence on Directing Administrations

Directing administrations, vital for keeping up with natural equilibrium, are unpredictably connected to biodiversity. Woodlands, going about as carbon sinks, assume a fundamental part in directing the worldwide environment. Deforestation and the deficiency of different plant species compromise this limit, adding to the amassing of ozone harming substances in the air and fueling environmental change.

Wetlands, with their capacity to channel and filter water, are fundamental for managing water quality. The deficiency of wetlands, frequently depleted for horticulture or metropolitan turn of events, lessens their ability to give clean water and builds the dangers of floods and dry seasons.

The decay of pollinators, including honey bees and butterflies, influences the fertilization of yields and wild plants, affecting the development of organic products, vegetables, and seeds. This influences food accessibility as well as disturbs environments and the untamed life that depends on these plants for food.

Influence on Social Administrations

Social administrations, attached to the tasteful, sporting, and otherworldly worth of environments, are significantly impacted by biodiversity misfortune. The debasement of normal scenes, the vanishing of notable species, and the deficiency of biodiversity-rich regions decrease the open doors for social and sporting encounters.

Public stops and safeguarded regions, intended to save biodiversity and give spaces to individuals to interface with nature, face expanded tension from environment annihilation, obtrusive species, and environmental change. The deficiency of biodiversity inside these region undermines their capacity to satisfy social and sporting capabilities.

Influence on Supporting Administrations

Supporting administrations, fundamental for keeping up with the circumstances essential forever, are straightforwardly affected by the wellbeing of biodiversity. Soil ripeness, for example, depends on the presence of different microbial networks, bugs, and plant species. The deficiency of these parts through territory annihilation and contamination prompts debased soils, diminished horticultural efficiency, and expanded weakness to disintegration. Biodiversity misfortune likewise influences supplement cycling, a basic interaction for the working of environments. The deterioration of natural matter, worked with by assorted microbial networks and detritivores, discharges fundamental supplements once again into the dirt. The downfall of biodiversity disturbs this cycle, prompting irregular characteristics in supplement accessibility and compromising the general strength of biological systems.

5. Preservation and Rebuilding Techniques

Resolving the mind boggling issue of biodiversity misfortune requires a multi-layered approach that joins preservation endeavors, feasible asset the board, and strategy mediations. A few systems can assist with relieving the effects of biodiversity misfortune and add to the rebuilding of environments:

Safeguarded Regions and Preservation Stores

Laying out and really overseeing safeguarded regions and preservation holds is basic for defending biodiversity. These regions give territories to various species, safeguard biological systems from disastrous exercises, and act as communities for logical exploration and natural training.

Economical Land Use Practices

Advancing maintainable land use rehearses, for example, agroforestry, natural cultivating, and manageable ranger service, helps preserve biodiversity while addressing human requirements. These practices plan to adjust the utilization of regular assets with the support of sound environments, lessening the effect of farming and ranger service on biodiversity.

Territory Reclamation

Endeavors to reestablish debased environments, whether through reforestation, wetland rebuilding, or coral reef restoration, add to the recuperation of biodiversity. Living space reclamation projects intend to reproduce conditions reasonable for local species, permitting environments to recuperate and work all the more successfully.

Maintainable Fisheries The board

Carrying out economical fisheries the board works on, including managing fishing portions, safeguarding basic territories, and decreasing bycatch, keeps up with fish populaces and safeguard marine biodiversity. Embracing environment based ways to deal with fisheries the executives thinks about the interconnections among species and their natural surroundings.

Intrusive Species The executives

Controlling and forestalling the spread of obtrusive species is fundamental for safeguarding local biodiversity. This incorporates checking and early location of intrusions, executing measures to forestall presentations, and utilizing systems for the evacuation or control of laid out obtrusive species.

Environmental Change Moderation

Moderating environmental change is pivotal for diminishing the dangers presented to biodiversity. This includes progressing to environmentally friendly power sources, advancing energy productivity, and executing strategies that limit ozone harming substance emanations. Worldwide participation, as exemplified by arrangements like the Paris Understanding, assumes a key part in tending to the worldwide test of environmental change.

Instruction and Mindfulness

Bringing issues to light about the significance of biodiversity and its job in biological system administrations is fundamental for encouraging a feeling of stewardship among networks. Training programs, public effort drives, and the coordination of biodiversity preservation into school educational plans add to building a general public that qualities and effectively takes part in the security of biodiversity.

2.1 Role of Biodiversity in Ecosystem Resilience

Biodiversity, the assortment of life on The planet, is a critical determinant of environment versatility — the limit of biological systems to endure and recuperate from unsettling influences. Environments, going from lavish rainforests to parched deserts, are dynamic and continually presented to different stressors, including environmental change, natural surroundings misfortune, and human exercises. The perplexing connections between various species and their surroundings add to the solidness and flexibility of environments. In this investigation, we will dive into the basic job that biodiversity plays in improving environment versatility and the expansive ramifications for the prosperity of the planet.

1. **Biodiversity and Environment Working**

    Biodiversity is a proportion of the range of species, qualities, and environments inside a given district. Biological systems are made out of a huge number of animal varieties, each with one of a kind qualities and jobs. The connections between these species add to the working of environments, impacting cycles like supplement cycling, fertilization, and decay.

    Supplement Cycling

    Biodiversity is fundamental for supplement cycling, the interaction by which fundamental components like carbon, nitrogen, and phosphorus travel through biological systems. Various types of microorganisms, plants, and creatures assume explicit parts in supplement cycling. For instance, decomposer creatures separate natural matter into supplements that can be consumed by plants, advancing the development of vegetation. The variety of species guarantees the proficiency and strength of supplement cycles, making environments more hearty despite aggravations.

Fertilization

Many plant species depend on pollinators like honey bees, butterflies, and birds for generation. Biodiversity, especially concerning pollinator species, is urgent for guaranteeing effective fertilization and the development of products of the soil. Various pollinator networks upgrade the strength of environments by giving overt repetitiveness — on the off chance that one animal types declines because of an unsettling influence, others might possibly fill the hole.

Bother Control

Savage species assume a crucial part in controlling herbivore populaces, forestalling overgrazing and keeping up with the equilibrium of biological systems. Biodiversity upgrades the viability of bug control by supporting various hunters that target various herbivores.

This regular guideline assists environments with recuperating from aggravations and forestalls the predominance of specific species that could adversely affect biological system elements.

2. **Biological system Versatility and Soundness**

Biological system versatility alludes to the capacity of an environment to assimilate and recuperate from aggravations while keeping up with its design and capability. Biodiversity is a key component impacting the flexibility and steadiness of biological systems, and a few instruments feature the interconnected connection between the two.

Overt repetitiveness and Practical Variety

Biodiversity gives overt repetitiveness in biological capabilities, implying that various species perform comparative jobs inside an environment. On the off chance that one animal types is harmed by an unsettling influence, different species with comparative capabilities can redress, forestalling a breakdown in biological system administrations. This overt repetitiveness improves the security and strength of biological systems by guaranteeing that fundamental capabilities endure even despite ecological changes. Utilitarian variety, which alludes to the range of biological capabilities performed by various species, is one more basic part of environment flexibility. Various environments are bound to contain species with a scope of utilitarian characteristics, permitting them to adjust to evolving conditions. For example, in a woods, different tree species might have fluctuating resiliences to dry season or protection from bothers. This variety of characteristics adds to the general strength of the timberland biological system.

Obstruction and Strength to Aggravations

Biodiversity adds to both the obstruction and flexibility of biological systems notwithstanding aggravations. Opposition alludes to the capacity of a biological system to endure an unsettling influence without going through huge changes, while flexibility is the capacity to recuperate and get back to a steady state after an unsettling influence.

High biodiversity can improve opposition by circulating dangers across various species and utilitarian gatherings. On the off chance that an unsettling influence, for example, a sickness episode or outrageous climate occasion, influences a specific animal varieties, others might stay unaffected, keeping up with in general biological system capability. Furthermore, the presence of different species improves the probability that a will have characteristics that give protection from explicit unsettling influences.

Strength, then again, depends on the limit of biological systems to recuperate after unsettling influences. Biodiversity adds to versatility by supporting a different cluster of animal types with various life history techniques, development rates, and regenerative examples. This variety permits biological systems to recuperate all the more quickly as species with high conceptive limit may rapidly recolonize upset regions.

3. **Biodiversity and Environmental Change Strength**

Environmental change represents a critical danger to biological systems around the world, with climbing temperatures, modified precipitation examples, and outrageous climate occasions testing the versatility of species and environments. Biodiversity assumes a basic part in improving the flexibility of environments to environmental change influences.

Temperature Guideline

Various biological systems, especially woodlands, add to temperature guideline through cycles like happening and concealing. Happening, the arrival of water fume from plant leaves, meaningfully affects the climate. The shade given by assorted plant shelters manages temperatures on the backwoods floor. Biodiversity guarantees that various species can flourish under differing temperature conditions, adding to the general temperature guideline limit of environments.

Transformation and Relocation

As environment conditions change, a few animal varieties might have to move their reaches to follow reasonable environments. Biodiversity gives the vital unrefined substance to variation through the presence of hereditary variety inside populaces. Species with different genetic stocks have a higher probability of containing people with characteristics that give resistance to evolving conditions. This hereditary variety is vital for the drawn out versatility of species and environments.

Also, environments with high biodiversity offer more choices for species to relocate and track down reasonable natural surroundings. Halls associating different territories work with the development of species, permitting them to follow changes in environment and find new regions helpful for their endurance. This availability is imperative for forestalling separation and upgrading the versatility of species.

Carbon Sequestration

Woodlands, with their rich biodiversity, are urgent players in carbon sequestration — the most common way of catching and putting away air carbon dioxide. Different tree species have extraordinary capacities with respect to carbon capacity, and various woods will generally sequester more carbon than monocultures. The deficiency of biodiversity, especially through deforestation, compromises the capacity of environments to sequester carbon, adding to the development of ozone harming substances in the air and fueling environmental change.

4. **Human Prosperity and Biodiversity**

The association among biodiversity and environment versatility straightforwardly influences human prosperity. Biological system administrations got from biodiverse environments are fundamental for food security, clean water, environment guideline, and social and sporting encounters.

Food Security

Biodiversity is basic for worldwide food security, as it guarantees the accessibility of different yields and animals. Horticultural frameworks that depend on different yields and hereditary assets are stronger to vermin, illnesses, and changing natural circumstances. Hereditary variety in plant and creature species adds to the advancement of strong and useful farming frameworks, defending food supplies for developing populaces.

Medication and Drugs

The rich variety of plant and microbial species fills in as a tremendous asset for the improvement of drugs and drugs. Numerous conventional prescriptions and current medications are gotten from intensifies tracked down in different plant and creature species. The deficiency of biodiversity decreases the potential for finding new helpful specialists, restricting our capacity to address arising wellbeing challenges.

Environment Guideline and Calamity Avoidance

Biodiverse environments assume a vital part in controlling environment designs, impacting precipitation, and relieving the effect of outrageous climate occasions. Woods, wetlands, and mangroves go about as regular supports against floods, storms, and different debacles. The deficiency of biodiversity diminishes the limit of environments to offer these administrative types of assistance, expanding the weakness of human networks to environment related chances.

Social and Sporting Qualities

Biodiversity adds to the social and sporting upsides of scenes. Normal regions wealthy in biodiversity, for example, public parks and natural life saves, are repositories of environmental variety as well as spaces for social and sporting encounters. The deficiency of biodiversity reduces the amazing open doors for individuals to associate with nature, influencing the prosperity of people and networks.

5. **Protection and Rebuilding Procedures for Improving Biological system Versatility**

Rationing and reestablishing biodiversity is fundamental for upgrading environment flexibility and guaranteeing the proceeded with arrangement of biological system administrations. A few techniques can be utilized to accomplish these objectives:

Safeguarded Regions and Preservation Stores

Laying out and really overseeing safeguarded regions and protection saves are critical for defending biodiversity. These regions act as shelters for different species, permitting them to endure notwithstanding environment misfortune and different dangers. All around planned safeguarded regions likewise add to availability, working with the development of species and advancing hereditary variety.

Manageable Land Use Practices

Advancing economical land use rehearses, for example, agroforestry, natural cultivating, and manageable ranger service, helps moderate biodiversity while addressing human requirements. These practices plan to adjust the utilization of normal assets with the upkeep of sound biological systems, decreasing the effect of farming and ranger service on biodiversity.

Territory Rebuilding

Endeavors to reestablish corrupted natural surroundings, whether through reforestation, wetland reclamation, or coral reef restoration, add to the recuperation of biodiversity. Environment rebuilding projects expect to reproduce conditions reasonable for local species, permitting biological systems to recuperate and work all the more actually.

Environmental Change Moderation

Moderating environmental change is fundamental for lessening the dangers presented to biodiversity. This includes progressing to environmentally friendly power sources, advancing energy effectiveness, and carrying out strategies that limit ozone harming substance discharges. Worldwide collaboration, as exemplified by arrangements like the Paris Understanding, assumes a key part in tending to the worldwide test of environmental change.

Obtrusive Species The executives

Controlling and forestalling the spread of intrusive species is fundamental for safeguarding local biodiversity. This incorporates observing and early location of attacks, executing measures to forestall presentations, and utilizing systems for the evacuation or control of laid out intrusive species.

Local area Commitment and Training

Including neighborhood networks in protection endeavors and giving schooling on the significance of biodiversity encourages a feeling of stewardship. Local area drove drives, for example, feasible asset the executives and resident science programs, add to the assurance of biodiversity and upgrade the strength of biological systems.

2.2Consequences of Biodiversity Decline

The continuous decrease in biodiversity, driven by human exercises, for example, territory obliteration, contamination, environmental change, and overexploitation of regular assets, has significant and sweeping ramifications for biological systems, human prosperity, and the soundness of the planet. As the complex snare of life unwinds, coming up next are a portion of the huge outcomes of biodiversity decline:

Environment Flimsiness:

Biodiversity is a vital figure keeping up with the strength and versatility of biological systems. As species vanish, biological systems become more defenseless against aggravations like sicknesses, intrusive species, and outrageous climate occasions. Decreased biodiversity lessens the capacity of biological systems to adjust and recuperate, making them more defenseless to environmental lopsided characteristics and interruptions.

Loss of Biological system Administrations:

Environments give many administrations fundamental for human endurance and prosperity. From food creation and clean water to environment guideline and infectious prevention, these administrations rely upon biodiversity. The downfall of species and environments compromises the limit of nature to convey these administrations, straightforwardly influencing human social orders and economies.

Influence on Food Security:

Biodiversity misfortune compromises worldwide food security. Many yields depend on pollinators like honey bees, butterflies, and birds for effective generation. The decay of pollinator species imperils crop yields and the development of products of the soil. Furthermore, the deficiency of hereditary variety in crops decreases the versatility of farming frameworks, making them more helpless to nuisances, illnesses, and changing ecological circumstances.

Diminished Strength to Environmental Change:

Biodiversity assumes a pivotal part in aiding environments adjust to and moderate the effects of environmental change.

Different biological systems, especially timberlands, go about as carbon sinks, sequestering carbon dioxide and directing environment designs. The deficiency of biodiversity lessens the capacity of biological systems to adapt to evolving temperatures, changed precipitation designs, and other environment related stressors.

Diminished Therapeutic Assets:

Many plants and microorganisms add to the improvement of prescriptions and drugs. Biodiversity misfortune lessens the pool of likely remedial specialists, restricting our capacity to find new medications. Native and conventional information on restorative plants, frequently firmly connected to biodiversity, is additionally in danger of being lost.

Social and Sporting Effects:

Biodiversity decline influences the social and sporting qualities related with normal scenes. Notorious species, different environments, and safeguarded regions add to the social personality of networks and give spaces to sporting encounters. The deficiency of biodiversity lessens these amazing open doors, affecting the prosperity of people and networks.

Expanded Weakness to Cataclysmic events:

Biodiverse biological systems, like mangroves, wetlands, and woodlands, go about as regular supports against cataclysmic events. They give assurance from floods, tempests, and torrents. The downfall of biodiversity lessens the limit of environments to offer these defensive administrations, expanding the weakness of human networks to the effects of catastrophic events.

Monetary Expenses:

Biodiversity misfortune accompanies critical monetary expenses. The downfall of biological systems that help fisheries, farming, and the travel industry straightforwardly influences jobs and economies. The requirement for fake substitutes for environment administrations, like fertilization or water cleaning, can prompt inflated costs for human social orders.

Loss of Hereditary Assets:

Biodiversity envelops hereditary variety inside species, giving the natural substance to transformation and advancement. The deficiency of species implies the deficiency of extraordinary hereditary qualities that could be important for creating versatile yields, fighting illnesses, and tending to different difficulties.

Disturbance of Biological Connections:

Species inside environments frequently have complex connections, including hunter prey cooperations and harmonious conditions. The deficiency of one animal categories can disturb these connections, prompting flowing impacts all through the biological system. This can bring about populace blasts of specific species, overgrazing, and different uneven characters.

2.3 Importance of Ecosystem Services

Environment benefits, the different advantages that people get from biological systems, assume a principal part in supporting life on The planet. These administrations, given by the mind boggling snare of living creatures and their surroundings, are fundamental for human prosperity, monetary flourishing, and the working of social orders. Understanding and perceiving the significance of environment administrations is essential for informed navigation, maintainable asset the board, and the protection of biodiversity.

Provisioning Administrations:

Provisioning administrations include the substantial items that environments accommodate human utilization. This incorporates food assets like natural products, vegetables, grains, and fish. Biological systems additionally offer unrefined components like lumber, filaments, and therapeutic plants. The variety of species and biological systems adds to a wide cluster of provisioning administrations, guaranteeing a practical stock of fundamental assets for human social orders.

Managing Administrations:

Managing administrations include the control of regular cycles that straightforwardly influence human prosperity. Environments assume a key part in environment guideline by engrossing carbon dioxide, settling temperatures, and impacting precipitation designs. Wetlands and backwoods add to water cleaning, shielding human populaces from waterborne illnesses. Environments likewise direct bugs and infections, decreasing the requirement for engineered pesticides and adding to horticultural supportability.

Social Administrations:

Social administrations include the non-material advantages that biological systems give, adding to the social and sporting parts of human existence. Picturesque scenes, biodiversity-rich regions, and safeguarded regular spaces offer open doors for tasteful delight, profound reflection, and sporting exercises. Public parks, untamed life stores, and regular milestones hold social importance and add to the personality of networks.

Supporting Administrations:

Supporting administrations are the fundamental cycles that keep up with the circumstances important for life on The planet. These incorporate supplement cycling, soil arrangement, and biodiversity itself. Biological systems, through assorted communications among species, add to the versatility and flexibility of the planet. The strength of supporting administrations is fundamental for the coherence of other environment administrations.

Biodiversity Preservation:

Environment administrations are complicatedly connected to biodiversity. The variety of species inside biological systems guarantees the arrangement of many administrations. Biodiversity adds to the security and strength of biological systems, improving their capacity to endure aggravations. Protection endeavors pointed toward safeguarding biodiversity straightforwardly add to the maintainability of biological system administrations.

Monetary Worth:

Biological system administrations have critical monetary worth, frequently misjudged in conventional financial models. Businesses like farming, fisheries, and ranger service straightforwardly rely upon provisioning administrations. The travel industry area benefits from social administrations, attracting guests to assorted and environmentally rich regions. The monetary prosperity of networks is personally attached to the maintainable utilization of biological system administrations.

Perceiving the significance of environment administrations is indispensable to taking on maintainable practices and arrangements. As human exercises progressively influence environments, understanding the worth of the administrations they give becomes principal to cultivating an amicable concurrence among social orders and the normal world. Supportable improvement requires an all encompassing methodology that recognizes the perplexing connections between biodiversity, environments, and the prosperity of current and people in the future. By focusing on the protection and supportable administration of biological systems, humankind can guarantee the proceeded with accessibility of fundamental administrations that support life on The planet.

Chapter 3

Conservation Strategies In A Changing Climate

As the effects of environmental change become progressively apparent, the field of preservation faces uncommon difficulties. The changing environment adjusts biological systems, disturbs living spaces, and compromises the endurance of innumerable species. Protection methodologies should adjust to this new reality, incorporating environment flexibility into the conservation of biodiversity. This far reaching investigation digs into key protection systems pointed toward relieving the impacts of environmental change on environments and species.

1. **Understanding the Environmental Change Danger**

   Environmental change represents a multi-layered danger to biodiversity, influencing biological systems across the globe. Increasing temperatures, changed precipitation designs, outrageous climate occasions, and ocean level ascent are among the climatic movements that straightforwardly influence species and territories. These progressions add to territory misfortune, disturbances in movement designs, and expanded weakness to sicknesses and obtrusive species. Understanding the particular dangers presented by environmental change is a central stage in creating compelling protection methodologies.

Living space Misfortune and Discontinuity:

One of the most quick and noticeable effects of environmental change is the adjustment of territories. Climbing temperatures might compel species to relocate to higher rises or scopes looking for appropriate environments. In any case, many scenes are divided by human framework, making it provoking for species to move and track down new natural surroundings. This environment misfortune and discontinuity can prompt separation, lessening hereditary variety and upsetting the capacity of populaces to adjust.

Changing Precipitation Examples:

Adjusted precipitation designs add to dry spells, floods, and changes in water accessibility. Sea-going environments, specifically, are delicate to shifts in precipitation. Drying wetlands, adjusted stream streams, and changing sea conditions influence the rearing and taking care of grounds of various species.

Creatures of land and water, for instance, are exceptionally delicate to changes in water accessibility, and modified precipitation designs represent a huge danger to their endurance.

Sea Fermentation and Coral Blanching:

The retention of abundance carbon dioxide by the world's seas prompts sea fermentation, affecting marine life, especially living beings with calcium carbonate skeletons like corals. Coral dying, a peculiarity exacerbated by hotter sea temperatures, undermines the soundness of coral reefs. These energetic and various environments are essential for marine biodiversity and fisheries. The debasement of coral reefs has flowing consequences for the whole marine food web.

Outrageous Climate Occasions:

The recurrence and power of outrageous climate occasions, including storms, fierce blazes, and heatwaves, are expanding because of environmental change. These occasions can straightforwardly annihilate environments, upset biological systems, and lead to populace declines. Species that are now at the edge of their natural resilience are especially defenseless. For instance, fierce blazes can crush territories and drive species to the edge of eradication, particularly in locales with fire-delicate vegetation.

2. **Protection Systems in a Changing Environment**

To address the difficulties presented by environmental change, protection systems should be dynamic, versatile, and informed by the most recent logical examination. The accompanying key procedures frame an extensive way to deal with relieving the effects of environmental change on biodiversity.

Safeguarded Regions and Availability:

Fortifying and growing safeguarded regions is a foundation of preservation endeavors. Safeguarded regions act as shelters for species, giving secure environments where they can flourish. Be that as it may, taking into account availability between safeguarded areas is significant. Making environmental halls permits species to move between natural surroundings, working with relocation and hereditary trade. This is especially significant as species might have to move their reaches to follow reasonable environments.

Environment Strong Assignments:

While laying out safeguarded regions, taking into account their environment resilience is fundamental. This includes distinguishing regions that are probably going to stay reasonable for species as the environment changes.

Assigning environment versatile regions guarantees that preservation endeavors have a higher probability of outcome in the long haul. Preservation associations and policymakers ought to team up to integrate environment strength into the preparation and the board of safeguarded regions.

Helped Movement and Movement:

As environmental change modifies the geographic appropriation of species, moderates might think about helped movement or movement endeavors. These include deliberately moving species to regions where they are anticipated to flourish from here on out. While questionable, particularly while including imperiled species, these methodologies plan to upgrade the versatile limit of species confronting quick environmental change. Cautious preparation, checking, and moral contemplations are essential in executing such mediations.

Natural surroundings Rebuilding and The executives:

Reestablishing debased environments and carrying out successful natural surroundings the executives rehearses add to the versatility of biological systems. This incorporates reforestation, wetland reclamation, and manageable land-use rehearses. Reestablished territories give basic asylums to species and upgrade the general strength of biological systems. Rebuilding endeavors ought to consider environment projections to guarantee that reestablished territories stay reasonable notwithstanding continuous environmental change.

Environment Informed Protection Arranging:

Protection arranging should integrate environmental change contemplations all along. Using environment models and situation arranging recognizes regions liable to be affected and directs the choice of protection needs. Environment informed preservation arranging incorporates evaluating the weakness of species, recognizing potential environment refugia, and creating methodologies to safeguard basic natural surroundings.

Hereditary Variety Preservation:

Keeping up with hereditary variety inside populaces is significant for the versatility of species to evolving conditions. Protection endeavors ought to focus on the safeguarding of assorted genetic stocks, particularly for species in danger of populace declines. Hostage reproducing programs, seed banks, and other hereditary protection drives assist with shielding the hereditary variety vital for species to develop and adjust to new ecological difficulties.

Local area Based Preservation:

Connecting with neighborhood networks in preservation endeavors is fundamental for the achievement and supportability of drives. Nearby information and customary practices can contribute significant experiences into the changing elements of biological systems. Furthermore, engaging networks to partake in preservation encourages a feeling of stewardship and guarantees that protection procedures line up with the requirements and desires of individuals living in and around safeguarded regions.

Environment Brilliant Protection Strategies:

Policymakers assume a vital part in supporting environment savvy protection drives. Carrying out arrangements that address the main drivers of environmental change, like lessening ozone harming substance discharges, is indispensable to the progress of protection endeavors. Environment savvy strategies additionally incorporate boosting maintainable land-use works on, advancing sustainable power, and coordinating environment contemplations into land-use arranging.

3. **Difficulties and Contemplations**

While these preservation procedures give a structure to tending to the effects of environmental change on biodiversity, a few difficulties and contemplations should be considered:

Moral Contemplations:

Preservation mediations, like helped relocation or movement, raise moral issues. Moving species to new regions might have unseen side-effects, and the potential for upsetting existing environments should be painstakingly assessed. Moral contemplations likewise stretch out to the removal of nearby networks and the potential for accidental effects on native information and social practices.

Asset Impediments:

Protection endeavors are many times compelled by restricted assets, both monetary and human. Carrying out enormous scope preservation systems requires significant interests in examination, observing, and on-the-ground exercises. Cooperation between state run administrations, non-legislative associations, and the confidential area is significant to actually assemble assets.

Eccentric Environmental Reactions:

The intricacy of environments makes foreseeing their reactions to preservation intercessions testing. Species might display surprising ways of behaving, and the outcome of preservation systems might rely upon a scope of natural variables.

Versatile administration, continuous observing, and a readiness to change techniques in view of new data are fundamental parts of effective preservation in an evolving environment.

Human-Untamed life Struggle:

As species shift their reaches because of environmental change, clashes with human populaces might increment. Creatures entering new regions looking for reasonable living spaces might come into contact with agribusiness, metropolitan regions, or framework, prompting human-untamed life clashes. Tending to these contentions requires compelling methodologies for concurrence and economical land-use arranging.

Worldwide Cooperation:

Numerous species have ranges that cross public boundaries, requiring worldwide coordinated effort for viable preservation. Environmental change is a worldwide test that requires facilitated endeavors between nations. Arrangements, like the Show on Natural Variety, give systems to global joint effort in the preservation of biodiversity.

Public Mindfulness and Training:

Building public mindfulness and comprehension of the effects of environmental change on biodiversity is fundamental. Educated and drawn in networks are bound to help protection endeavors and supporter for arrangements that address the underlying drivers of environmental change. Training programs, outreach drives, and correspondence methodologies assume an essential part in encouraging a feeling of obligation and stewardship.

3.1 Adaptive Management Approaches

Versatile administration is an iterative and adaptable way to deal with preservation and asset the executives that recognizes the inborn vulnerability in complex biological systems. Despite dynamic and erratic ecological changes, versatile administration systems give a structure to gaining from progressing protection endeavors, changing techniques in view of new data, and working on the strength of environments. This exhaustive investigation dives into the standards, key parts, and uses of versatile administration draws near, accentuating their significance in tending to the developing difficulties of biodiversity preservation.

1. **Standards of Versatile Administration**

   Versatile administration is directed by a bunch of rules that recognize it from more conventional, static administration draws near. These standards mirror a guarantee to embracing vulnerability, advancing learning, and encouraging strength in protection endeavors.

   Iterative Interaction:

   Versatile administration is portrayed by its repeating and iterative nature. It includes arranging, carrying out, checking, and rethinking preservation systems in a constant circle. The cycle takes into consideration changes in light of the criticism and bits of knowledge acquired from observing and assessment.

   Learning and Trial and error:

   The methodology supports a culture of learning and trial and error. Preservation specialists effectively try to work on how they might interpret environments by testing speculations, investigating different administration intercessions, and adjusting techniques in view of noticed results. This accentuation on learning upgrades the versatile limit of preservation programs.

Adaptability and Flexibility:

Versatile administration embraces the comprehension that circumstances and settings can change after some time. Protection systems are intended to be adaptable and movable, considering changes in light of unexpected difficulties or open doors. This adaptability guarantees that administration rehearses stay important and compelling notwithstanding developing natural circumstances.

Cooperative Independent direction:

Viable versatile administration includes joint effort among assorted partners, including researchers, neighborhood networks, policymakers, and preservation specialists. The coordination of alternate points of view and information frameworks upgrades the heartiness of dynamic cycles and encourages shared responsibility for drives.

Unequivocal Suspicions and Theories:

Versatile administration requires the unequivocal explanation of presumptions and speculations fundamental preservation methodologies. By making these suppositions unequivocal, experts can methodallly test them through observing and change methodologies in light of the arising proof. This straightforwardness upgrades the logical meticulousness of versatile administration.

Checking and Assessment:

Checking is a focal part of versatile administration, giving the information expected to evaluate the results of protection intercessions. Thorough and deliberate assessment permits professionals to measure the progress of systems, distinguish regions for development, and settle on informed conclusions about whether to keep up with, change, or leave explicit methodologies.

2. **Key Parts of Versatile Administration**

Versatile administration includes a few key parts that all in all add to its viability in tending to the intricacies of protection challenges. These parts are interconnected and support each other inside the iterative pattern of versatile administration.

Organized Direction:

The course of versatile administration starts with organized direction, where preservation goals, the executives choices, and the hidden suppositions are unequivocally characterized. This stage requires input from partners, including researchers, policymakers, and neighborhood networks. By deliberately framing objectives and systems, professionals establish the groundwork for ensuing checking and learning.

Checking and Information Assortment:

Hearty observing is a foundation of versatile administration. It includes the orderly assortment of information to evaluate the results of preservation mediations. Checking endeavors ought to line up with the goals and suppositions framed during the organized dynamic stage. Information assortment strategies might incorporate field studies, remote detecting, and local area based perceptions, contingent upon the particular objectives of the preservation program.

Learning and Input:

Versatile administration focuses on gaining from the results of preservation activities. Criticism instruments are fundamental for making an interpretation of checking information into significant bits of knowledge. Experts dissect the aftereffects of their intercessions, contrast them with anticipated results, and recognize examples or patterns that illuminate ensuing independent direction. This constant learning circle improves the versatile limit of protection drives.

Choice Investigation and Change:

Choice investigation includes blending checking information, assessing the presentation of protection systems, and arriving at informed conclusions about changes. This stage requires a basic assessment of the presumptions and speculations directing the underlying choices. Professionals might decide to keep up with viable systems, adjust those that are less effective, or investigate completely new methodologies in light of the aggregated information.

Correspondence and Coordinated effort:

Viable correspondence is pivotal all through the versatile administration process. Straightforwardness about direction, observing outcomes, and changes constructs trust among partners. Joint effort guarantees that different viewpoints are thought of, and shared learning upgrades the aggregate capacity to answer arising difficulties.

Institutional Help:

Fruitful execution of versatile administration needs institutional help. This incorporates cultivating a culture that values development, trial and error, and nonstop improvement. Satisfactory subsidizing, preparing, and limit building drives add to the drawn out progress of versatile administration programs.

3. **Utilizations of Versatile Administration in Preservation**

Versatile administration approaches track down application across different preservation settings, from safeguarded region the executives to feasible fisheries and environment rebuilding. The adaptability and responsiveness of versatile administration make it especially appropriate to address the vulnerabilities and dynamic nature of protection challenges.

Safeguarded Region The executives:

Safeguarded regions are fundamental for saving biodiversity, however they face various dangers, including living space corruption, environmental change, and human-natural life struggle. Versatile administration permits safeguarded region administrators to persistently survey the viability of preservation systems, change limits or the board rehearses, and answer changing biological circumstances.

Maintainable Fisheries:

Fisheries the board is intrinsically intricate, with vulnerabilities connected with fish stocks, environment elements, and financial variables. Versatile administration in fisheries includes setting harvest limits in view of logical evaluations, observing fish populaces and environment wellbeing, and changing administration measures on a case by case basis. This approach forestalls overfishing and upholds the drawn out supportability of fisheries.

Environment Reclamation:

Reestablishing debased environments frequently includes vulnerabilities about the progress of intercessions and the flexibility of biological systems to outside pressures.

Versatile administration in environment reclamation permits specialists to explore different avenues regarding different rebuilding methods, screen the recuperation of vegetation and natural life, and refine systems in view of noticed results. This iterative interaction improves the probability of effective rebuilding results.

Environmental Change Variation:

Environmental change adds an extra layer of intricacy to preservation endeavors. Versatile administration gives a structure to tending to the vulnerabilities related with changing environment conditions. Protection projects can constantly evaluate the effects of environmental change on species and biological systems, change natural surroundings the executives rehearses, and investigate novel ways to deal with upgrade the strength of biodiversity to an evolving environment.

Local area Based Preservation:

Versatile administration is especially important in local area based preservation drives, where nearby networks assume a focal part in navigation. By consolidating neighborhood information and drawing in networks in observing and assessment, versatile administration guarantees that preservation systems line up with the necessities and desires of individuals living in and around safeguarded regions.

4. **Difficulties and Reactions**

While versatile administration offers a dynamic and responsive way to deal with protection, it isn't without difficulties and reactions. Tending to these worries is urgent for refining and reinforcing versatile administration procedures.

Information Restrictions:

Sufficient checking depends on strong information, and at times, information might be restricted or testing to get. This is especially evident in remote or understudied environments. Deficient or erroneous information can think twice about adequacy of versatile administration, underscoring the requirement for creative information assortment techniques and expanded interest in checking foundation.

Time and Asset Imperatives:

Versatile administration demands significant investment and assets, both concerning information assortment and examination. In circumstances where protection experts acknowledgment or spending plan imperatives, the full execution of versatile administration might challenge. Adjusting the requirement for exhaustive checking with viable contemplations is a continuous test.

Protection from Change:

Executing versatile administration might experience opposition inside associations or among partners who are acclimated with additional customary, hierarchical methodologies. Embracing a culture of trial and error and learning requires a change in outlook, and conquering protection from change can be a critical obstruction to the reception of versatile administration.

Scale Confuse:

The scale at which versatile administration is carried out should match the size of natural cycles and preservation challenges. Befuddles between the size of the board activities and the size of natural cycles can restrict the adequacy of versatile administration. This features the significance of considering spatial and transient scales while planning and carrying out versatile administration techniques.

Moral Contemplations:

Versatile administration mediations might have moral ramifications, particularly when they include trial and error with imperiled species or environments. Adjusting the possible advantages of learning and further developing preservation results with moral contemplations, for example, the prosperity of individual creatures or biological systems, requires cautious idea and thought.

Absence of Consistency:

The eccentric idea of biological frameworks implies that results can't necessarily be dependably anticipated, even with thorough checking and investigation. The absence of consistency can be trying for chiefs and may prompt dissatisfaction or suspicion about the adequacy of versatile administration.

3.2 Restoration and Rehabilitation Techniques

Reclamation and recovery are essential parts of biodiversity protection, meaning to switch or alleviate the effects of human exercises, natural surroundings debasement, and ecological aggravations. These methods include purposeful mediations to reestablish biological systems to a more regular or practical state, improving biodiversity, environment administrations, and by and large natural strength. This investigation dives into key rebuilding and restoration strategies, underlining their significance in cultivating the recuperation of biological systems and advancing maintainable collaborations among people and the climate.

1. **Natural Rebuilding**

   Natural rebuilding is a thorough methodology zeroed in on reestablishing the construction, capability, and biodiversity of environments that have been corrupted or changed. The accompanying strategies are usually utilized in environmental rebuilding endeavors:

   Local Species Renewed introduction:

   Once again introducing local plant and creature species is a major part of environmental rebuilding. This procedure revamps different and versatile biological systems by reestablishing species that have been lost because of territory obliteration or other human exercises. Cautious thought is given to choosing species that are all around adjusted to the particular environmental states of the reclamation site.

Territory Recreation:

Territory recreation includes remaking the actual design of environments, like wetlands, timberlands, or meadows. This might incorporate restoring regular geography, water stream examples, or vegetation cover. Reproduction endeavors plan to make conditions that help the arrival of local species and advance the recuperation of biological system processes.

Soil Remediation:

Soil debasement is a typical outcome of human exercises, influencing the soundness of biological systems. Soil remediation methods, for example, adding natural matter, establishing cover yields, or utilizing mycorrhizal parasites, are utilized to further develop soil construction, richness, and supplement content. Sound soils are fundamental for supporting plant development and supporting assorted natural networks.

Control of Intrusive Species:

Intrusive species can outcompete and uproot local widely varied vegetation, adding to biological system debasement. Biological rebuilding frequently includes the control or expulsion of intrusive species to make space for the recuperation of local biodiversity. Methodologies might incorporate manual expulsion, natural control techniques, or the utilization of designated herbicides.

Hydrological Rebuilding:

Numerous biological systems, like wetlands and riparian regions, depend on unambiguous hydrological conditions for their wellbeing. Hydrological rebuilding includes overseeing water stream, levels, and examples to copy regular circumstances. This is especially significant in regions where human exercises, like dam development or land waste, have changed the regular hydrology.

2. Recovery Strategies

Recovery strategies center around working on the biological usefulness of debased environments without essentially reestablishing them to their unique state. These methodologies expect to upgrade the limit of biological systems to offer types of assistance and backing biodiversity. Normal recovery procedures include:

Agroforestry and Economical Land Use:

Incorporating trees and bushes into agrarian scenes through agroforestry rehearses adds to territory variety and further develops soil fruitfulness. Agroforestry frameworks advance practical land use, giving advantages to both biodiversity and nearby networks.

Revegetation and Reforestation:

Revegetation includes establishing vegetation in regions where it has been lost or debased. Reforestation explicitly focuses on the reclamation of timberlands. These methods assist with settling soil, improve water maintenance, and give territory to various species. Rebuilding endeavors frequently incorporate the utilization of local plant species to boost biological advantages.

Fake Reefs:

In marine conditions, where coral reefs and different environments are compromised, the arrangement of fake reefs can improve living space intricacy and backing the recuperation of marine life. These designs, frequently made of materials like cement or reused materials, give connection surfaces to coral and asylum for different marine species.

Hydroponics Best Practices:

Hydroponics, when overseen economically, can add to the recovery of sea-going biological systems. Executing best practices in hydroponics, for example, limiting territory obliteration, controlling supplement inputs, and staying away from the utilization of destructive synthetic substances, mitigates the adverse consequences of this action on encompassing environments.

Metropolitan Greening and Green Framework:

In metropolitan conditions, restoration procedures include consolidating green spaces and green framework. Establishing trees, making metropolitan stops, and carrying out green rooftops and walls add to biodiversity in urban communities, give living space to metropolitan natural life, and upgrade the general nature of the metropolitan climate.

3. Checking and Versatile Administration

No matter what the particular reclamation or restoration procedure utilized, constant observing and versatile administration are basic parts of accomplishment. Ordinary evaluations of the environmental reaction to intercessions assist specialists with understanding what is working and where changes are required. Versatile administration includes rolling out informed improvements to rebuilding or restoration methodologies in view of observing outcomes and arising information.

Benchmark Evaluations:

Prior to starting reclamation or recovery endeavors, gauge appraisals are led to figure out the present status of the environment. This incorporates studies of biodiversity, soil quality, hydrological conditions, and other important elements. Standard information give a reference highlight assessing the progress of mediations.

Long haul Observing:

Long haul observing includes consistently evaluating the recuperation of environments overstretched periods. This might remember following changes for vegetation creation, natural life populaces, soil wellbeing, and different pointers. Long haul checking distinguishes patterns, measure achievement, and illuminate versatile administration choices.

Versatile Administration Criticism Circle:

The versatile administration process includes a continuous criticism circle. As checking information opens up, professionals investigate the outcomes, recognize examples or difficulties, and make acclimations to reclamation or recovery procedures as needs be. This iterative cycle upgrades the viability of intercessions over the long haul.

Partner Commitment:

Drawing in partners, including neighborhood networks, researchers, and policymakers, in the checking and versatile administration process is significant. Neighborhood information contributes important experiences, and cooperative dynamic improves the achievement and manageability of reclamation and recovery drives.

3.3 Sustainable Land Use Planning

Practical land use arranging is a vital and comprehensive methodology that looks to adjust the contending requests of human turn of events and ecological preservation. It intends to upgrade the utilization of land assets while limiting adverse consequences on environments, biodiversity, and regular territories.

This multidisciplinary cycle thinks about friendly, financial, and natural elements to direct the dependable and fair utilization of land. Here, we investigate the key standards, parts, and advantages of supportable land use arranging.

1. **Standards of Maintainable Land Use Arranging**

   Coordinated Arranging:

   Feasible land use arranging accentuates a coordinated methodology that thinks about different elements, including ecological protection, financial turn of events, social value, and social contemplations. By incorporating these angles, organizers can foster thorough methodologies that address the assorted necessities of networks while protecting regular assets.

   Environment Based Approach:

   Perceiving the interconnectedness of biological systems, reasonable land use arranging focuses on an environment based approach. This includes considering the environmental capabilities and administrations given via scenes, safeguarding basic natural surroundings, and keeping up with biodiversity. It expects to figure out some kind of harmony that takes into account human exercises without compromising the respectability of environments.

Local area Commitment:

Comprehensive people group commitment is a central standard of practical land use arranging. It guarantees that neighborhood networks have a voice in dynamic cycles, considering the fuse of conventional information and local area desires. Connecting with partners cultivates a feeling of responsibility and advances the drawn out supportability of land use plans.

Versatile Administration:

Manageable land use arranging recognizes the powerful idea of social and environmental frameworks. The reception of versatile administration standards takes into account progressing checking, assessment, and change of land use procedures in light of evolving conditions, arising difficulties, and new data.

Conservation of Green Spaces:

The insurance of green spaces, like parks, normal stores, and horticultural terrains, is a critical guideline of manageable land use arranging. These regions add to biodiversity protection, give sporting open doors, and deal fundamental environment administrations, including air and water purging.

2. **Parts of Feasible Land Use Arranging**

Land Drafting and Guideline:

Compelling area drafting and guideline are fundamental to maintainable land use arranging. Drafting assigns explicit regions for various purposes, for example, private, business, modern, and preservation. Guidelines guide improvement exercises inside these zones, guaranteeing that they line up with supportability goals and natural assurance.

Biodiversity Halls:

Planning and keeping up with biodiversity halls is a urgent part of manageable land use arranging. These passageways associate divided natural surroundings, working with the development of untamed life and advancing hereditary variety. Biodiversity passageways upgrade biological system strength and assist species with adjusting to changing natural circumstances.

Shrewd Development Procedures:

Shrewd development procedures focus on smaller, blended use improvement to diminish endless suburbia. By moving advancement in existing metropolitan regions, practical land use arranging means to limit territory fracture, safeguard agrarian land, and advance productive land use.

Environment Responsive Preparation:

Given the effects of environmental change, supportable land use arranging consolidates environment responsive procedures. This incorporates recognizing regions powerless against environment related chances, like flooding or outrageous intensity, and executing measures to improve flexibility, for example, green framework and maintainable water the executives rehearses.

Feasible Farming Practices:

Empowering feasible agrarian practices is necessary to land use arranging. This includes advancing agroecological strategies, limiting the utilization of unsafe agrochemicals, and supporting differentiated and versatile cultivating frameworks. Economical horticulture adds to food security while decreasing negative natural effects.

3. **Advantages of Economical Land Use Arranging**

Preservation of Environment Administrations:

Manageable land use arranging shields fundamental biological system administrations, including clean water arrangement, air quality guideline, and environment guideline. By protecting normal regions and limiting natural surroundings annihilation, these administrations keep on helping both human networks and the climate.

Biodiversity Protection:

Through the foundation of safeguarded regions, biodiversity halls, and green spaces, maintainable land use arranging adds to the protection of biodiversity. This, thusly, upholds the wellbeing and versatility of environments and the species they support.

Upgraded Personal satisfaction:

Very much arranged networks, with admittance to green spaces, sporting facilities, and economical framework, add to an improved personal satisfaction for occupants. Manageable land use arranging advances walkable areas, public transportation, and a feeling of local area prosperity.

Environmental Change Moderation and Transformation:

Practical land use arranging assumes a part in environmental change relief and transformation. By diminishing ozone depleting substance discharges related with never-ending suburbia, protecting carbon sinks, and consolidating environment responsive procedures, it adds to the worldwide work to address environmental change.

Social Value:

The consideration of local area partners in the arranging system guarantees that land use choices think about friendly value. Manageable land use arranging tries to address abberations in admittance to assets, foundation, and ecological advantages, advancing reasonableness and inclusivity.

4. **Difficulties and Contemplations**

Irreconcilable situation:

Supportable land use arranging frequently includes exploring irreconcilable situations among partners with disparate needs. Adjusting financial turn of events, protection, and local area needs requires powerful exchange and split the difference.

Political Will and Strategy Execution:

The progress of economical land use arranging depends on political will and the viable execution of strategies. Difficulties might emerge on the off chance that there is inadequate help from policymakers or on the other hand assuming administrative systems need implementation instruments.

Information Accessibility and Limit:

Reasonable land use arranging expects admittance to exact and exceptional information on biological systems, land use, and social elements. In certain districts, information accessibility might be restricted, and there might be an absence of limit with respect to extensive preparation.

Transient versus Long haul Contemplations:

Adjusting transient advancement objectives with long haul maintainability targets can challenge. Strain for sure fire monetary increases might struggle with the requirement for economical, tough land use rehearses that benefit people in the future.

4

Chapter 4

Policy Frameworks For Climate-Resilient Ecosystems

As the effects of environmental change become progressively obvious, the requirement for hearty strategy structures to shield and upgrade the strength of biological systems is more earnest than any other time. Environmental change presents uncommon difficulties to biodiversity, biological system administrations, and the prosperity of networks subject to normal assets. This extensive investigation digs into the vital components of strategy structures for environment strong biological systems, analyzing the difficulties, open doors, and best practices in exploring this basic convergence of ecological preservation and environment transformation.

1. **Understanding the Environmental Change Danger to Biological systems**
Temperature Limits:
Increasing worldwide temperatures are adjusting the essential climatic circumstances that biological systems depend on. Temperature limits, including heatwaves and delayed times of raised temperatures, can prompt weight on plant and creature species,

upsetting biological equilibriums and pushing a few animal categories past their resilience limits.

Changing Precipitation Examples:

Environmental change is additionally reshaping precipitation designs, prompting more extraordinary and flighty precipitation in certain locales and broadened dry seasons in others. These progressions influence water accessibility, soil dampness, and the wellbeing of sea-going biological systems, influencing the dispersion and overflow of species reliant upon explicit hydrological conditions.

Ocean Level Ascent and Beach front Disintegration:

The warming environment adds to the dissolving of polar ice covers and ice sheets, bringing about ocean level ascent. Waterfront biological systems face the double danger of rising oceans and expanded storm floods, prompting environment misfortune, salinization of freshwater assets, and expanded weakness for networks living in beach front regions.

Sea Fermentation:

The assimilation of overabundance carbon dioxide by the world's seas prompts sea fermentation, especially influencing marine environments. Fermentation represents a danger to marine existence with calcium carbonate skeletons, like corals and mollusks, influencing the design of coral reefs and the wellbeing of marine biodiversity.

Outrageous Climate Occasions:

The recurrence and force of outrageous climate occasions, including typhoons, out of control fires, and floods, are on the ascent because of environmental change. These occasions can bring about far and wide territory obliteration, loss of biodiversity, and interruptions to environment capabilities, prompting long haul ramifications for both normal and human frameworks.

2. **Key Parts of Strategy Systems for Environment Tough Biological systems**

Environment Tough Safeguarded Regions:

Reinforcing and growing safeguarded regions is a foundation of strategy systems for environment tough environments. Safeguarded regions act as shelters for biodiversity, giving territories where species can flourish. Nonetheless, these regions should be planned and dealt in light of environment flexibility, taking into account factors like territory availability, rise angles, and the capacity of species to relocate in light of evolving conditions.

Environment Based Variation (EbA):

Environment Based Variation (EbA) is a methodology that uses the intrinsic strength of biological systems to improve the capacity of both nature and individuals to adjust to environmental change. Strategy structures that advance EbA perceive the significance of solid biological systems in offering fundamental types of assistance, like water decontamination, flood guideline, and soil adjustment, which add to the general strength of networks.

Green Framework Advancement:

Green framework includes the essential utilization of regular frameworks, like wetlands, backwoods, and green spaces, to address environmental change influences. Strategy systems can boost the improvement of green framework in metropolitan preparation, transportation, and water the board. This approach improves environment versatility by advancing regular arrangements that give numerous advantages to the two biological systems and human social orders.

Environment Savvy Agribusiness:

Horticulture is profoundly defenseless against environmental change, with influences on crop yields, water accessibility, and soil wellbeing. Strategy structures for environment tough biological systems ought to consolidate environment shrewd horticultural practices. This incorporates advancing manageable cultivating techniques, agroforestry, and the utilization of environment safe yield assortments that can adjust to changing natural circumstances.

Local area Based Protection and Variation:

Drawing in nearby networks in protection and variation endeavors is fundamental. Strategy systems ought to help local area based approaches that coordinate conventional information and practices. Nearby people group are much of the time the first to encounter the effects of environmental change, and their association is significant for the achievement and supportability of biological system strength drives.

Coordinated Water Asset The board:

Water is a basic part of biological systems, and environmental change can essentially modify water accessibility and quality. Incorporated Water Asset The board (IWRM) arrangements consider the whole water cycle, from source to the ocean, and expect to adjust contending water needs while safeguarding the well-being of amphibian environments. Viable water the board is basic to environment versatility across different scenes.

Supportable Ranger service Practices:

Woodlands assume a significant part in sequestering carbon, keeping up with biodiversity, and managing water cycles. Reasonable ranger service rehearses, directed by strategy structures, guarantee that woods are overseen such that improves flexibility to environmental change. This incorporates manageable logging, reforestation endeavors, and security against out of control fire chances.

3. **Challenges in Executing Strategy Structures**

Political Will and Responsibility:

One of the essential difficulties in executing strategy structures for environment versatile biological systems is the requirement for supported political will and responsibility. Powerful arrangements require long haul arranging, and political advances or changing needs can block the congruity and progress of preservation and transformation drives.

Cross-Sectoral Coordination:

Biological systems are interconnected, and environment flexibility requires coordination across different areas, including climate, farming, water the board, and metropolitan preparation. Accomplishing cross-sectoral coordination can be trying because of disparate interests, contending needs, and varying ways to deal with administration.

Restricted Monetary Assets:

Executing environment versatile arrangements frequently requires critical monetary assets. Numerous areas, especially those generally helpless against environmental change, may confront constraints in financing for protection and variation drives. Preparing monetary assets, both locally and globally, is a basic part of beating this test.

Information and Information Holes:

Compelling arrangement advancement depends on precise and cutting-edge information. In any case, in numerous districts, there are critical holes in information connected with biodiversity, environment effects, and biological system administrations. Tending to these information holes is fundamental for going with informed choices and planning strategies that genuinely improve environment flexibility.

Discriminatory Effects on Weak People group:

Weak people group, frequently those with restricted assets and social strength, are excessively impacted by environmental change. Carrying out strategy systems should think about the potential for biased influences and endeavor to guarantee that variation and protection endeavors don't worsen existing social abberations.

Compromises and Irreconcilable situations:

Adjusting the contending interests of financial turn of events, protection, and environment variation can prompt compromises and irreconcilable situations. For instance, rural extension might be financially helpful yet could come to the detriment of regular living spaces. Policymakers should explore these intricacies to find arrangements that line up with various targets.

4. **Worldwide Coordinated effort and Systems**
The Paris Understanding:
The Paris Understanding, embraced in 2015 under the Unified Countries Structure Show on Environmental Change (UN-FCCC), addresses a milestone global work to address environmental change. While it fundamentally centers around moderating ozone depleting substance emanations, its accentuation on variation and strength lines up with the more extensive objectives of environment tough biological systems.

Nations are urged to incorporate biological system based approaches in their Broadly Resolved Commitments (NDCs).

Show on Organic Variety (CBD):
The CBD is a worldwide deal that tends to the protection of biodiversity and the practical utilization of natural assets. The CBD perceives the reliance of biodiversity and environmental change and underlines the significance of biological system based transformation and protection procedures. The Post-2020 Worldwide Biodiversity Structure, as of now under exchange, is supposed to assume a urgent part in adjusting biodiversity and environment objectives.

Intergovernmental Board on Environmental Change (IPCC):
The IPCC gives logical evaluations of environmental change effects, variation, and relief. Its reports illuminate policymakers and add to the improvement of worldwide systems. IPCC evaluations feature the interconnectedness of environmental change and biodiversity misfortune, building up the requirement for coordinated approaches in strategy advancement.

Worldwide Climate Office (GEF):
The GEF is a monetary component that supports ventures and drives advancing worldwide ecological advantages, including biodiversity protection and environmental change variation.

It works with worldwide participation and gives subsidizing to projects that incorporate environment flexibility and biological system protection.

5. **Contextual investigations: Representing Successful Approach Structures**

Costa Rica's Installment for Environment Administrations (PES) Program:

Costa Rica's PES program is an effective illustration of a strategy structure that adjusts monetary motivations to natural protection. The program pays landowners for keeping up with and reestablishing backwoods, advancing supportable land use rehearses, and adding to carbon sequestration. This drive plays had a huge impact in safeguarding the country's rich biodiversity.

Germany's Public Transformation System:

Germany's Public Variation Methodology frames a far reaching way to deal with environment versatility, including areas like horticulture, ranger service, water the executives, and biodiversity. The methodology accentuates the significance of biological systems in adjusting to environmental change and incorporates measures to upgrade environment versatility, safeguard biodiversity, and advance maintainable land use rehearses.

Australia's Extraordinary Hindrance Reef Versatility System:

The Incomparable Boundary Reef Versatility Procedure is intended to upgrade the flexibility of the world's biggest coral reef framework to environmental change influences. The system incorporates measures to diminish nearby stressors, further develop water quality, and backing the recuperation of coral environments. It coordinates environment transformation with preservation endeavors, perceiving the interconnected idea of biological system wellbeing and environment versatility.

4.1 International Agreements and Protocols

Even with squeezing worldwide natural difficulties, countries have perceived the basic for cooperative activity to resolve issues, for example, environmental change, biodiversity misfortune, and the corruption of biological systems. Peaceful accords and conventions act as essential structures that empower nations to meet up, share liabilities, and work toward shared objectives. This investigation dives into key peaceful accords and conventions, analyzing their importance, triumphs, challenges, and the developing scene of worldwide ecological collaboration.

1. **Verifiable Setting and Importance**
   The Stockholm Gathering (1972):
   The Stockholm Gathering on the Human Climate, held in 1972, denoted a defining moment in global natural collaboration. It was the principal worldwide meeting of its sort, uniting delegates from 113 nations to talk about natural issues. The gathering prompted the foundation of the Assembled Countries Climate Program (UNEP) and laid the basis for future global ecological arrangements.
   The Structure Show on Environmental Change (1992):
   The Unified Countries System Show on Environmental Change (UNFCCC), took on in 1992, addresses a milestone peaceful accord pointed toward tending to environmental change. The show sets out a structure for intergovernmental endeavors to balance out ozone harming substance focuses in the environment, with a definitive target of forestalling hazardous anthropogenic impedance with the environment framework.
   The Show on Organic Variety (1992):
   The Show on Organic Variety (CBD), likewise settled in 1992, is an extensive system for the preservation and reasonable utilization of biodiversity. With the three fundamental targets of preservation, maintainable use, and the fair and evenhanded sharing of advantages, the CBD plays had a pivotal impact in directing worldwide endeavors to safeguard the rich variety of life on The planet.

2. **Key Peaceful accords and Conventions**

The Kyoto Convention (1997):

Expanding on the UNFCCC, the Kyoto Convention, took on in 1997, set restricting discharge decrease focuses for created nations. It addressed a critical stage in perceiving and tending to the separated liabilities of created and emerging countries with regards to environmental change. The convention presented market-based components, for example, outflows exchanging and the Perfect Improvement System (CDM), to upgrade adaptability in gathering targets.

The Paris Arrangement (2015):

The Paris Understanding, took on in 2015, is a milestone global accord that expands on the establishment laid by the UNFCCC. It expects to restrict worldwide temperature increment well under 2 degrees Celsius above pre-modern levels, with endeavors to restrict the increment to 1.5 degrees Celsius. The arrangement underlines broadly resolved commitments (NDCs), mirroring every country's obligation to lessening discharges and upgrading environment strength.

The Nagoya Convention on Admittance to Hereditary Assets and the Fair and Impartial Sharing of Advantages Emerging from their Use (2010):

As a beneficial consent to the CBD, the Nagoya Convention tends to the fair and evenhanded sharing of advantages emerging from the use of hereditary assets. It gives a structure to admittance to hereditary assets, benefit-sharing, and consistence. The convention recognizes the significance of customary information on native and nearby networks in the preservation and manageable utilization of organic variety.

The Montreal Convention on Substances that Exhaust the Ozone Layer (1987):

The Montreal Convention, embraced in 1987, is a global arrangement intended to safeguard the ozone layer by getting rid of the creation and utilization of ozone-exhausting substances (ODS). It is hailed as perhaps of the best natural understanding, displaying the worldwide local area's capacity to cooperatively resolve a squeezing ecological issue. The convention's alterations have prompted critical decreases in the utilization of ODS, adding to the recuperation of the ozone layer.

The Ramsar Show on Wetlands (1971):

The Ramsar Show, embraced in 1971, is a global settlement committed to the protection and practical utilization of wetlands. Wetlands are indispensable environments that offer various natural types of assistance, including water sanitization, flood control, and territory for different greenery. The show underlines the significance of perceiving the worth of wetlands and advancing their protection on a worldwide scale.

The Cartagena Convention on Biosafety (2000):

The Cartagena Convention, a valuable consent to the CBD, addresses the protected exchange, dealing with, and utilization of living changed creatures (LMOs) coming about because of present day biotechnology. It intends to guarantee the protected treatment of hereditarily altered creatures (GMOs) and their items to forestall unfavorable impacts on natural variety, considering the dangers to human wellbeing.

3. **Victories and Accomplishments**

Ozone Layer Security:

The Montreal Convention's progress in eliminating ozone-exhausting substances is a demonstration of the viability of global participation. The convention has prompted a continuous recuperation of the ozone layer, showing the way that deliberate worldwide endeavors can address complex ecological difficulties.

Environment Arrangements and the Paris Understanding:

The Paris Understanding addresses a critical accomplishment in the domain of environmental change moderation and variation. Its comprehensive nature, permitting every country to decide its commitments, encourages a feeling of shared liability. The understanding's accentuation on restricting worldwide temperature increments and supporting non-industrial countries in their environment activities mirrors a complete and ground breaking approach.

Preservation of Biodiversity:

The CBD, alongside its valuable conventions like the Nagoya Convention, plays had a urgent impact in progressing worldwide endeavors to monitor biodiversity. Through public techniques, safeguarded regions, and drives for supportable asset use, the show has added to the security of environments and the advancement of biodiversity protection.

Wetland Protection:

The Ramsar Show has been effective in bringing issues to light about the environmental significance of wetlands. Through the assignment of Ramsar Locales and the execution of the executives designs, the show has worked with the protection and astute utilization of wetlands around the world.

Economical Administration of Hereditary Assets:

The Nagoya Convention tends to the fair and evenhanded sharing of advantages got from the use of hereditary assets. By perceiving the worth of conventional information and laying out standards for benefit-sharing, the convention adds to the feasible administration of hereditary assets, cultivating participation among suppliers and clients.

4. **Difficulties and Reactions**

Absence of Implementation Components:

Numerous peaceful accords and conventions need powerful requirement systems. While these arrangements put forth out aggressive objectives and responsibilities, the shortfall of compelling components to guarantee consistence can subvert their general effect. Non-restricting nature and powerless requirement have been refered to as constraints in accomplishing the ideal results.

Varying Public Needs and Responsibilities:

Countries frequently have differing needs and responsibilities, prompting difficulties in arriving at agreement and executing worldwide ecological arrangements. Variations in financial turn of events, asset accessibility, and international interests can thwart brought together activity and weaken the viability of peaceful accords.

Deficient Subsidizing and Assets:

Execution of ecological arrangements requires monetary assets, mechanical help, and limit building endeavors, especially for agricultural countries. Deficient financing and assets can hinder the capacity of nations, particularly those with restricted limits, to satisfy their responsibilities and actually add to worldwide ecological objectives.

Intricacy and Extensive Exchange Cycles:

The exchange and confirmation processes for peaceful accords can be extended and complex. The different interests of partaking nations, the requirement for agreement, and the complexities of legitimate and specialized viewpoints add to delayed dealings. The lengthy course of events might ruin opportune reactions to dire natural difficulties.

Deficient Incorporation of Native People groups and Nearby People group:

The job of native people groups and neighborhood networks in ecological preservation is many times deficiently perceived in peaceful accords. Their customary information and maintainable practices are significant for biodiversity protection and environment flexibility. A more comprehensive methodology that consolidates the points of view and privileges of these networks is fundamental for powerful natural administration.

5. **Advancing Scene: Arising Issues and Future Possibilities**

Incorporation of Environment and Biodiversity Plans:

There is a developing acknowledgment of the interconnectedness between environmental change and biodiversity misfortune. Endeavors are in progress to coordinate environment and biodiversity plans, recognizing that resolving one issue disregarding the other may prompt fragmented arrangements. The Post-2020 Worldwide Biodiversity Structure is supposed to add to this incorporation.

Accentuation on Nature-Based Arrangements:

The idea of nature-based arrangements (NbS) has acquired noticeable quality as a methodology that use the force of nature to address ecological difficulties. Peaceful accords are progressively consolidating NbS, perceiving the job of biological systems in giving savvy and economical answers for environmental change, biodiversity misfortune, and other natural issues.

Calls for Additional Aggressive Targets:

Considering the speeding up speed of ecological corruption, there are calls for additional aggressive targets and responsibilities in peaceful accords. The earnestness of tending to environmental change and biodiversity misfortune has incited conversations on putting forth more aggressive objectives that line up with the size of the difficulties.

Worldwide Flexibility Drives:

Endeavors to fabricate worldwide versatility to natural difficulties are getting forward movement. These drives center around improving the flexibility of biological systems, networks, and economies notwithstanding environment related influences. Peaceful accords are supposed to progressively integrate flexibility incorporating measures into their structures.

Advanced Innovations and Natural Observing:

Progressions in advanced advancements, including satellite observing, remote detecting, and huge information examination, are changing ecological checking and requirement. These advances upgrade the capacity to follow and survey natural changes, screen consistence with arrangements, and backing proof based independent direction.

4.2 National and Local Legislation

Public and neighborhood regulation assumes a urgent part in molding the system for ecological administration, giving the legitimate establishment to the security, protection, and manageable utilization of normal assets. These regulations act as fundamental devices in tending to natural difficulties, controlling human exercises, and advancing an agreeable connection among society and the environments whereupon it depends. This investigation dives into the meaning of public and neighborhood regulation in natural administration, looking at their jobs, viability, and the difficulties related with their execution.

1. **Public Regulation: Making way for Ecological Insurance Production of Legitimate Structures:**

   Public regulation gives the legitimate foundation important to natural insurance and the executives. Nations authorize regulations that lay out the expectations of people, organizations, and government elements concerning the climate. These structures articulate the core values, principles, and requirement systems to guarantee the economical utilization of normal assets.

   Natural Effect Appraisal (EIA):

   Numerous countries require Natural Effect Evaluations (EIAs) as a feature of the regulative cycle for improvement projects. EIAs assess the likely ecological results of proposed exercises, assisting chiefs with pursuing informed decisions that offset advancement objectives with natural assurance. This official instrument encourages a proactive way to deal with manageable turn of events.

   Safeguarded Regions and Biodiversity Protection:

   Public regulation frequently assigns safeguarded regions, for example, public parks, untamed life stores, and protection regions, to shield biodiversity and basic biological systems. These regulations frame guidelines for exercises inside these areas, planning to save novel living spaces, safeguard imperiled species, and keep up with natural equilibrium.

   Air and Water Quality Norms:

Regulation lays out norms for air and water quality, addressing contaminations and emanations that posture dangers to human wellbeing and the climate. Administrative systems put down certain boundaries on the arrival of contaminations, advance contamination anticipation gauges, and endorse punishments for rebelliousness, adding to the insurance of environments and public prosperity.

Squander The board and Reusing:

Public regulations administer squander the executives works on, illustrating methodology for garbage removal, reusing, and unsafe waste treatment. These guidelines plan to limit the natural effect of waste and empower feasible waste administration works on, accentuating the significance of the roundabout economy.

2. **Neighborhood Regulation: Fitting Answers for Local area Needs**

Drafting and Land Use Arranging:

Neighborhood regulation, frequently through drafting mandates, guides land use arranging inside networks. These regulations decide the proper utilization of land for private, business, modern, and preservation purposes.

Drafting forestalls random turn of events, safeguard regular natural surroundings, and make spaces for local area amusement.

Local area Ecological Strategies:

Neighborhood states can authorize explicit natural approaches custom-made to the one of a kind requirements and difficulties of their networks. These arrangements might resolve issues like air and water quality, commotion contamination, and green space protection. Nearby regulation permits networks to play a proactive job in molding their natural future.

Local area Based Protection Drives:

A few districts execute local area based protection drives through neighborhood regulation. These endeavors include coordinated effort between neighborhood networks, state run administrations, and non-legislative associations to economically oversee normal assets. Such drives perceive the significance of including networks in the dynamic cycle and utilizing nearby information for viable protection.

Metropolitan Greening and Feasible Turn of events:

Neighborhood regulation can advance metropolitan greening drives, empowering the improvement of green spaces, parks, and manageable framework inside urban areas. These endeavors upgrade the personal satisfaction for inhabitants, alleviate the metropolitan intensity island impact, and add to in general ecological strength.

Ecological Instruction and Mindfulness Projects:

Neighborhood regulation might uphold natural instruction and mindfulness programs inside networks. By integrating ecological educational program into schools, coordinating local area studios, and advancing mindfulness crusades, neighborhood states can cultivate a culture of natural obligation and supportability.

3. **Viability and Difficulties**

Compelling Execution and Authorization:

The viability of public and neighborhood natural regulation depends on strong execution and requirement components. Satisfactory assets, observing frameworks, and administrative offices are fundamental to immediately guarantee consistence and address infringement. Successful implementation cultivates a culture of responsibility and discourages naturally hurtful practices.

Public Cooperation and Mindfulness:

Effective ecological regulation frequently includes dynamic public investment and mindfulness. Drawing in networks in dynamic cycles, guaranteeing straightforwardness, and elevating ecological schooling add to a more educated and enabled populace. Regulation that reflects local area values and concerns is bound to acquire backing and consistence.

Interconnectedness of Neighborhood and Public Endeavors:

The outcome of ecological administration depends on the interconnectedness of neighborhood and public endeavors. Public regulation sets general principles, while nearby regulation fits these norms to address explicit local area needs. Powerful coordination among public and neighborhood levels guarantees an exhaustive and incorporated way to deal with ecological administration.

Limit Building and Asset Assignment:

Limit working at both public and nearby levels is pivotal for the viable execution of natural regulation. State run administrations should put resources into preparing projects, innovation, and ability to enable administrative bodies and neighborhood specialists. Satisfactory asset allotment guarantees that ecological regulations are authorized as well as effectively implemented.

Difficulties of Cross-Line Issues:

Ecological difficulties frequently rise above public and nearby limits. Issues like air and water contamination, biodiversity misfortune, and environmental change require global collaboration. Public and nearby regulation might confront difficulties in tending to cross-line ecological issues, featuring the requirement for cooperative systems and conciliatory endeavors.

4. **Peaceful accords and Arrangement with Public Regulation**

Public and nearby ecological regulation frequently lines up with and is impacted by peaceful accords and conventions. Nations that are involved with worldwide natural deals might integrate the standards and responsibilities of these arrangements into their homegrown regulations. This arrangement fortifies the lucidness and viability of natural administration on both public and global levels.

4.3 Integrating Climate Adaptation into Conservation Policies

As the effects of environmental change become progressively articulated, protection arrangements should advance to address the dynamic and interconnected difficulties confronting biological systems.

Incorporating environment transformation into protection procedures is foremost to guarantee the versatility of biodiversity and the drawn out practicality of biological systems. This investigation dives into the significance of adjusting protection arrangements to environment variation measures, inspecting key contemplations, effective methodologies, and the cooperative endeavors expected to shield the planet's normal legacy.

1. **The Interconnectedness of Environmental Change and Protection**

   Changing Environmental Circumstances:

   Environmental change is adjusting the essential natural circumstances that numerous species rely upon. Changes in temperature, precipitation designs, and the recurrence of outrageous climate occasions can disturb biological systems, affecting the appropriation, conduct, and wealth of plant and creature species.

   Biodiversity Misfortune:

   Environmental change compounds existing dangers to biodiversity, prompting living space misfortune, adjusted movement designs, and expanded weakness to illnesses. Preservation arrangements that don't represent these environment related stressors might miss the mark in safeguarding the wealth and variety of life on The planet.

   Environment Administrations Under Strain:

   Environmental change puts extra weight on the biological system benefits that networks depend on, like water cleaning, fertilization, and environment guideline. Preservation endeavors should consider the strength of environments to environment effects on guarantee the proceeded with arrangement of these basic administrations.

2. **Key Contemplations in Coordinating Environment Transformation into Protection Approaches**

   Evaluating Weakness and Strength:

Protection strategies need to integrate evaluations of weakness and strength to environmental change. Figuring out which species, living spaces, and biological systems are most in danger focuses on preservation activities. Recognizing versatile regions can direct endeavors to safeguard and reestablish environments equipped for enduring environment influences.

Dynamic Protection Arranging:

Customary preservation designs frequently expect a static climate. Despite environmental change, arrangements should embrace dynamic arranging approaches that record for moving species dispersions, changing relocation designs, and the requirement for natural surroundings passages that work with species development in light of environment shifts.

Consolidating Environment Science:

Protection strategies ought to be educated by the most recent environment science. This incorporates projections of future environment conditions, the recognizable proof of environment refugia, and the appraisal of possible changes in species conduct. Consolidating such logical experiences guarantees that protection procedures are versatile and forward-looking.

Local area Commitment and Versatile Administration:

Environment variation in preservation isn't exclusively a specialized test; it requires the dynamic commitment of nearby networks and versatile administration structures. Arrangements ought to encourage cooperation with networks, native people groups, and partners, incorporating customary information with logical experiences to upgrade the versatile limit of biological systems.

Saving Hereditary Variety:

Protection strategies should address the significance of saving hereditary variety inside species. This hereditary variety gives the natural substance to variation to changing ecological circumstances. Guaranteeing the strength of populaces to environment stressors includes keeping up with assorted genetic stocks through proper protection measures.

3. **Effective Ways to deal with Environment Versatile Protection Arrangements**

Environment Savvy Safeguarded Regions:

Upgrading the environment strength of safeguarded regions is pivotal. This includes growing safeguarded regions as well as guaranteeing that current ones are intended to endure environment influences. Network between safeguarded regions, permitting species to move in light of environment shifts, is a critical part of environment brilliant preservation.

Rebuilding and Environment Improvement:

Rebuilding endeavors that emphasis on improving environment versatility can contribute fundamentally to environment versatile protection.

Establishing local species, reestablishing wetlands, and executing maintainable land the executives practices can work on the limit of environments to adapt to environment related stressors.

Environment Based Variation (EbA):

Environment Based Variation (EbA) incorporates the utilization of biodiversity and biological system administrations into environment transformation procedures. Preservation approaches embracing EbA perceive that sound biological systems add to both environment flexibility and the prosperity of networks. Models incorporate safeguarding mangroves for beach front versatility and keeping up with in one piece timberlands for water guideline.

Versatile Hallway Arranging:

Making hallways that associate divided environments permits species to move and adjust to evolving conditions. Preservation approaches that focus on the foundation and assurance of versatile passageways add to keeping up with hereditary variety and supporting environment flexibility.

Motivators for Environment Tough Practices:
Arrangements that boost environment tough land use rehearses advance protection and transformation all the while. This might incorporate giving monetary impetuses to economical horticulture, agroforestry, and other land the board rehearses that upgrade biological system flexibility.

4. **Cooperative Endeavors and Worldwide Collaboration**
Worldwide Associations:
Environment versatile preservation strategies frequently require global coordinated effort. Worldwide associations can work with the trading of information, assets, and best practices. Cooperative endeavors empower nations to share encounters, coordinate protection procedures across borders, and on the whole location the transboundary effects of environmental change.

Arrangement with Peaceful accords:
Incorporating environment transformation into protection arrangements lines up with peaceful accords like the Paris Understanding and the Show on Organic Variety (CBD). Nations focused on these arrangements are urged to synchronize their protection endeavors with their environment activity plans, cultivating cognizance in tending to interconnected natural difficulties.

Limit Building and Innovation Move:
Cooperative endeavors ought to focus on limit building and the exchange of environment transformation advances. Supporting countries with restricted assets in creating and carrying out successful protection strategies upgrades their capacity to address environment influences on biodiversity and biological systems.

5. **Conquering Difficulties and Looking Forward**

Restricted Assets and Subsidizing:
Sufficient assets are fundamental for carrying out environment versatile protection approaches. Nations might confront difficulties in

getting subsidizing for checking, research, and on-the-ground protection endeavors. Worldwide monetary systems and organizations can assume an essential part in tending to asset limitations.

Strategy Coordination and Reconciliation:

Incorporating environment transformation into preservation arrangements requires coordination across different areas and government organizations. Defeating administrative storehouses and encouraging interdisciplinary joint effort are fundamental for creating comprehensive approaches that address the interconnected difficulties of environmental change and biodiversity misfortune.

Public Mindfulness and Instruction:

Fruitful execution of environment versatile preservation approaches depends on open mindfulness and schooling. Connecting with networks in understanding the linkages between environmental change and preservation cultivates a feeling of shared liability and supports neighborhood cooperation in protection endeavors.

Checking and Versatile Administration:

Normal observing of preservation results and versatile administration are basic parts of successful arrangements. Adaptability to change procedures in view of checking information guarantees that approaches stay receptive to changing circumstances and arising dangers.

5 |

Chapter 5

Community Involvement In Ecosystem Conservation

Environment protection is a worldwide goal, with the wellbeing and flexibility of biological systems straightforwardly connected to the prosperity of networks. Perceiving the multifaceted relationship between human social orders and the climate, the inclusion of nearby networks has arisen as a foundation of viable preservation procedures. This investigation digs into the multi-layered components of local area contribution in environment preservation, analyzing its importance, effective models, challenges, and the extraordinary capability of cooperative stewardship.

1. **Grasping the Significance of Local area Contribution in Environment Preservation**
   Neighborhood Information and Conventional Practices:
   Neighborhood people group frequently have priceless information about their biological systems, aggregated over ages. Customary practices, informed by this information, assume a significant part in keeping up with environmental equilibrium. Including people group guarantees the safeguarding of these works

on, improving the viability and maintainability of protection endeavors.

Stewardship and Feeling of responsibility:

At the point when networks effectively partake in the preservation of their neighborhood biological systems, a feeling of pride and stewardship arises. This profound association cultivates a drawn out obligation to safeguarding the climate. Networks become advocates for feasible practices and go about as gatekeepers of their biological legacy.

Financial and Job Advantages:

Protection endeavors that consider neighborhood financial and occupation needs are bound to acquire local area support. Reasonable asset the board practices can give monetary advantages through exercises like eco-the travel industry, manageable horticulture, and non-wood timberland items. This double spotlight on preservation and occupations makes a mutually beneficial situation.

Social and Social Importance:

Biological systems frequently hold social and social importance for neighborhood networks. Biodiverse scenes might be fundamental to social practices, ceremonies, and personalities. Drawing in networks in protection regards these social ties and guarantees that preservation systems line up with nearby qualities, cultivating an agreeable connection among individuals and the climate.

Tending to Natural Bad form:

Numerous people group, especially native and underestimated gatherings, endure the worst part of ecological corruption and environmental change. Including these networks in preservation involves natural equity. It engages them to address the effects of ecological changes and guarantees that preservation endeavors don't worsen existing disparities.

2. **Fruitful Models of Local area Contribution in Biological system Preservation**

Local area Based Regular Asset The executives (CBNRM):

CBNRM includes nearby networks in the feasible administration of regular assets. This model perceives the job of networks as caretakers of their surroundings and enables them to arrive at conclusions about asset use. Models incorporate local area oversaw fisheries, woods holds, and water catchment regions.

Participatory Preservation Arranging:

Drawing in networks in the arranging system guarantees that preservation procedures line up with nearby requirements and goals. Participatory methodologies include local area individuals in direction, permitting them to contribute customary information, recognize preservation needs, and co-plan procedures that are socially and environmentally significant.

Resident Science Drives:

Resident science draws in nearby networks in information assortment, checking, and research exercises. Local area individuals become dynamic members in logical undertakings, contributing significant information that illuminates protection procedures. This approach improves logical comprehension as well as fabricates a feeling of pride and obligation among members.

Local area Based Ecotourism:

Incorporating people group into ecotourism drives gives monetary impetuses to protection. Nearby occupants can become guides, hosts, or craftsmans, straightforwardly profiting from the travel industry while advancing the conservation of normal environments.

Very much planned ecotourism programs focus on local area inclusion and natural training.

Native and Customary Biological Information (TEK):

Perceiving and regarding native and customary biological information is vital to compelling preservation. Native people group frequently have profound experiences into nearby environments, including supportable asset the board rehearses. Incorporating TEK into preservation procedures improves logical comprehension and upgrades the significance of drives.

Local area Preservation Stores:

Laying out local area preservation saves engages neighborhood networks to oversee and safeguard assigned regions. These stores might zero in on biodiversity areas of interest, basic natural surroundings, or watershed regions. The contribution of networks in the preparation, checking, and implementation of guidelines guarantees the outcome of such drives.

3. **Challenges in Local area Association in Environment Preservation**

Restricted Assets and Limit:

Numerous people group, particularly those in asset compelled settings, miss the mark on monetary and specialized assets required for powerful preservation. Inadequate limit with respect to checking, research, and practical administration can thwart local area drove drives.

Clashing Interests and Needs:

Offsetting preservation objectives with the assorted interests and needs of networks can challenge. For example, financial constrains may lead networks to focus on momentary increases over long haul biological supportability. Successful correspondence and compromise are fundamental to exploring these pressures.

Absence of Lawful Acknowledgment and Land Residency Issues:

Insufficient lawful acknowledgment of local area land freedoms can sabotage protection endeavors. Land residency issues, including hazy property freedoms and infringement, may prompt living space corruption. Clear legitimate systems that perceive and safeguard local area privileges are critical for effective local area inclusion.

Social Imbalances and Power Elements:

Social disparities and power irregular characteristics inside networks can impact the conveyance of advantages and dynamic cycles.

Comprehensive methodologies that think about orientation elements, underestimated voices, and neighborhood power structures are fundamental for cultivating impartial local area association.

Outside Tensions and Double-dealing:

Outside factors, for example, market requests, worldwide exchange, and corporate interests, can apply tension on nearby networks and their environments. Unreasonable asset extraction, driven by outer interest, may think twice about drove preservation endeavors. Adjusting nearby and outside interests is a complex however fundamental part of effective local area inclusion.

Environmental Change Vulnerabilities:

The vulnerabilities related with environmental change represent extra difficulties. Networks might confront flighty changes in atmospheric conditions, influencing their customary information and business rehearses. Adjusting to these progressions needs continuous help, limit building, and cooperative endeavors.

4. **Procedures to Upgrade People group Association in Biological system Protection**

Limit Building and Training:

Engaging people group through schooling and limit building drives improves their capacity to take part in preservation effectively. Preparing in feasible asset the executives, checking methods, and natural training fabricates nearby mastery and cultivates a feeling of obligation.

Associations and Cooperation:

Coordinated effort between networks, government offices, non-legislative associations (NGOs), and scholarly establishments reinforces protection drives. Associations can give networks admittance to specialized skill, financing, and assets. Shared liability and cooperative dynamic upgrade the adequacy of protection endeavors.

Motivation Components for Protection:

Carrying out motivation systems, for example, installments for environment administrations (PES), guarantees that networks get unmistakable advantages from protection exercises. These motivating forces might incorporate monetary prizes, admittance to further developed foundation, or upgraded social administrations. Adjusting protection to nearby monetary interests encourages manageable practices.

Social Awareness and Regard:

Perceiving and regarding the social variety of networks is fundamental for fruitful preservation. Strategies and drives ought to be socially delicate, integrating customary practices and values. Building trust through conscious commitment improves the probability of local area purchase in.

Local area Strengthening and Consideration:

Engaging underestimated voices inside networks is pivotal for comprehensive protection. Drives ought to effectively try to incorporate ladies, native people groups, and other customarily underestimated gatherings. Local area drove dynamic cycles guarantee that assorted points of view add to preservation techniques.

Versatile Administration and Adaptability:

Protection techniques ought to embrace versatile administration standards, perceiving the unique idea of biological systems and networks. Adaptability in changing systems in light of observing information and local area criticism guarantees that drives stay receptive to changing circumstances and requirements.

Lawful Acknowledgment of Local area Privileges:

Clear legitimate systems that perceive and safeguard local area land and asset privileges are fundamental to fruitful preservation.

State run administrations ought to pursue lawful acknowledgment and residency security for networks, empowering them to oversee and ration their biological systems really.

5. **Groundbreaking Potential: People group Drove Preservation in the Anthropocene**

Flexibility Despite Worldwide Change:

Local area drove preservation exemplifies a strong way to deal with natural difficulties. Neighborhood people group, personally associated with their surroundings, are much of the time more versatile to change. Their customary information and practices, when coordinated with contemporary science, offer a comprehensive and versatile reaction to the intricacies of the Anthropocene.

Instructive and Support Job:

Local area association in preservation stretches out past the quick environment to training and support. Connected with networks become advocates for maintainable works on, impacting more extensive cultural perspectives toward preservation. This far reaching influence cultivates a culture of ecological stewardship that rises above nearby limits.

Safeguarding Social Legacy:

Local area association in protection guarantees the safeguarding of social legacy entwined with environments. Native information, narrating, and conventional practices add to a rich social embroidery that, when defended, turns into a wellspring of versatility and personality even with natural change.

Improving Versatile Administration:

Fruitful people group drove preservation improves versatile administration structures. Nearby dynamic cycles that integrate conventional information and local area viewpoints add to administration frameworks that are more responsive, comprehensive, and fit for tending to complex natural difficulties.

Advancing Supportable Ways of life:

Networks effectively took part in protection frequently take on maintainable ways of life that focus on concordance with nature. This shift toward maintainability stretches out past asset the board to envelop utilization designs, squander decrease, and a more extensive ethos of living in offset with the climate.

5.1 Engaging Local Communities

Drawing in nearby networks is a significant part of powerful natural preservation. The connection between human networks and the climate is multifaceted and interconnected, and including nearby occupants in protection endeavors guarantees a more all encompassing, supportable, and socially important methodology. This investigation digs into the meaning of drawing in nearby networks in natural protection, looking at the advantages, challenges, effective models, and key methodologies to cultivate significant support.

1. **Meaning of Connecting with Neighborhood People group in Preservation**

   Nearby Information and Mastery:

   Nearby people group frequently have an abundance of customary information and mastery about their surroundings. This information, collected over ages, envelops comprehension of nearby biological systems, weather conditions, and supportable asset the executives rehearses. Drawing in networks takes advantage of this important supply of astuteness, adding to more educated and setting explicit protection procedures.

   Social Association and Character:

   The social association that neighborhood networks have with their surroundings is significant. Environments frequently hold social importance, forming personalities, customs, and conviction frameworks.

   Drawing in networks in protection regards and use this social association, guaranteeing that preservation endeavors line up with nearby qualities and cultivate a feeling of social pride and character.

Local area Stewardship and Proprietorship:

Dynamic commitment encourages a feeling of stewardship and possession among nearby networks. At the point when occupants effectively take part in preservation drives, they become advocates for the assurance of their regular environmental factors. This feeling of pride adds to long haul responsibility and guarantees that networks assume a sense of ownership with the prosperity of their environments.

Maintainable Jobs:

Protection endeavors that consider nearby monetary requirements add to supportable vocations. Drawing in networks in exercises like practical farming, eco-the travel industry, and non-lumber backwoods item collecting can furnish monetary advantages while lining up with protection objectives. This double spotlight on ecological and financial maintainability makes a positive input circle.

Social Prosperity and Wellbeing:

Solid biological systems add to the prosperity and soundness of nearby networks. Clean air, water, and admittance to normal spaces are fundamental for physical and emotional wellness. Connecting with networks in preservation safeguards these imperative environment administrations as well as improves the general personal satisfaction for occupants.

2. **Advantages of Drawing in Nearby People group in Preservation**

Upgraded Preservation Results:

Neighborhood people group are in many cases best situated to figure out the complexities of their biological systems. Their cozy information on nearby vegetation, fauna, and natural elements can fundamentally improve the viability of preservation endeavors. Connecting with networks guarantees that preservation systems are customized to the particular necessities and difficulties of the neighborhood climate.

Local area Strengthening:

Connecting with neighborhood networks engages them to effectively partake in dynamic cycles. At the point when networks are engaged with forming protection strategies and practices, it encourages a feeling of organization and strengthening. Engaged people group are bound to take responsibility for drives and work cooperatively towards shared objectives.

Social Protection:

Protection endeavors that regard and include nearby networks add to the safeguarding of social legacy. Native practices, customary information, and social ceremonies frequently line up with feasible asset the executives. By drawing in with these social components, preservation drives safeguard biodiversity as well as protect social variety.

Social Attachment and Joint effort:

Cooperative protection drives fortify social union inside networks. At the point when occupants cooperate towards a shared objective, it fabricates a feeling of local area and collaboration. This social union is an important resource for tending to ecological difficulties and encouraging flexibility despite change.

Instructive Open doors:

Drawing in neighborhood networks in preservation gives instructive open doors to the two occupants and outer partners. Information trade between researchers, progressives, and local area individuals improves understanding and appreciation for the intricacies of nearby biological systems. This instructive viewpoint adds to building a local area that is ecologically proficient and effectively engaged with preservation.

3. **Challenges in Drawing in Nearby People group in Preservation**

   Correspondence Boundaries:

   Powerful commitment requires clear and socially touchy correspondence. Language obstructions, contrasts in correspondence styles, and differing levels of proficiency can present difficulties. Conquering these hindrances requires putting resources into compelling correspondence techniques and working with two-way exchange.

Clashing Needs and Interests:

Neighborhood people group frequently wrestle with a large number of needs and interests, including financial requirements, horticultural practices, and framework improvement. Offsetting preservation objectives with these contending interests can challenge. Distinguishing mutual benefit situations and adjusting protection endeavors to nearby needs is fundamental.

Restricted Assets and Limit:

Numerous neighborhood networks, especially in asset compelled settings, may miss the mark on monetary and specialized assets required for dynamic support in preservation drives. Deficient limit with regards to checking, research, and practical administration can impede significant commitment.

Power Elements and Disparity:

Power uneven characters inside networks, frequently affected by variables like orientation, standing, or financial status, can influence the evenhanded conveyance of advantages and dynamic cycles. Tending to these power elements is vital for guaranteeing that protection drives are comprehensive and advantage all local area individuals.

Outer Tensions and Double-dealing:

Outer variables, for example, worldwide market requests and corporate interests, can apply strain on nearby networks. Unreasonable asset extraction driven by outside request might think twice about drove protection endeavors. Safeguarding people group from abuse and guaranteeing fair advantage sharing are continuous difficulties.

Environmental Change Vulnerabilities:

The vulnerabilities related with environmental change add

intricacy to local area commitment. Networks might confront eccentric changes in weather conditions, influencing customary information and business rehearses. Adjusting to these progressions needs continuous help, limit building, and cooperative endeavors.

4. **Effective Models of Connecting with Neighborhood People group in Preservation**

Participatory Protection Arranging:

Participatory methodologies include local area individuals in the preparation and dynamic cycles of protection drives. This model guarantees that neighborhood information and points of view are incorporated into protection procedures, cultivating a feeling of responsibility and responsibility.

Local area Based Normal Asset The executives (CBNRM):

CBNRM includes neighborhood networks in the supportable administration of regular assets. This model perceives the job of networks as overseers of their surroundings and enables them to arrive at conclusions about asset use. Models incorporate local area oversaw fisheries, backwoods stores, and watershed security programs.

Resident Science Drives:

Resident science connects with neighborhood networks in information assortment, checking, and research exercises. Local area individuals become dynamic members in logical undertakings, contributing significant information that illuminates preservation methodologies. This approach improves logical comprehension as well as fabricates a feeling of pride and obligation among members.

Eco-accommodating Business Drives:

Drives that advance eco-accommodating livelihoods, like manageable farming, agroforestry, and eco-the travel industry, give financial motivators to preservation. By adjusting protection to neighborhood financial interests, these drives add to both natural and monetary supportability.

Native and Local area Oversaw Safeguarded Regions:

Perceiving and supporting native and local area oversaw safeguarded regions guarantees that preservation drives line up with nearby practices and needs. These regions frequently coordinate conventional environmental information with present day protection science, prompting viable and socially pertinent preservation results.

5. **Key Systems for Improving People group Commitment in Protection**

Local area Training and Mindfulness:

Building ecological education inside networks is principal to successful commitment. Instructive projects that impart the significance of biodiversity, environments, and reasonable practices engage local area individuals to partake in protection effectively.

Participatory Direction:

Including people group in dynamic cycles guarantees that their viewpoints are viewed as in the plan of protection arrangements. Participatory dynamic forms a feeling of pride and obligation, encouraging a cooperative way to deal with protection.

Social Awareness and Inclusivity:

Preservation drives should be socially touchy and comprehensive. Perceiving and regarding assorted social practices, values, and convictions guarantees that protection endeavors line up with neighborhood characters and needs.

Limit Building and Preparing:

Putting resources into the limit working of neighborhood networks improves their capacity to add to protection endeavors effectively. Preparing in maintainable asset the board, checking strategies, and other significant abilities engages networks to take on dynamic jobs in protection.

Motivator Systems:

Executing motivation instruments, for example, installments for environment administrations (PES), guarantees that networks get substantial advantages from preservation exercises. These motivations might incorporate monetary prizes, admittance to further developed framework, or improved social administrations.

Innovation and Development:

Utilizing innovation and creative arrangements can upgrade local area commitment in protection. Apparatuses, for example, portable applications for checking biodiversity, remote detecting for living space evaluation, and local area based planning engage networks with available and easy to use assets.

Cooperation and Organizations:

Cooperation between neighborhood networks, government offices, non-administrative associations (NGOs), and scholastic organizations reinforces preservation drives. Organizations can furnish networks with admittance to specialized skill, subsidizing, and assets, encouraging a cooperative and commonly useful methodology.

5.2 Indigenous Knowledge and Practices

Native information and practices, molded by ages of close collaboration with the normal world, comprise a rich and priceless asset for natural protection. These customary frameworks of understanding include a profound cognizance of environments, biodiversity, and reasonable asset the executives. This investigation dives into the meaning of native information, the remarkable viewpoints it offers, and how incorporating these practices into protection systems can upgrade both biological strength and social safeguarding.

1. **Meaning of Native Information in Preservation**
   All encompassing Comprehension of Biological systems:
   Native information frameworks frequently view biological systems in a comprehensive way, figuring out the interconnectedness of every living thing. This comprehensive viewpoint goes past a compartmentalized perspective on nature and thinks about the

complicated connections between plants, creatures, people, and the climate. Such an exhaustive comprehension is significant for viable preservation.

Biodiversity Preservation Practices:

Native people group have created complex strategies for saving biodiversity. Customary practices, like rotational cultivating, specific reaping, and local area oversaw safeguarded regions, are educated by a profound comprehension regarding environmental equilibrium. These practices add to the protection of assorted plant and creature species and keep up with the versatility of biological systems.

Feasible Asset The executives:

Native information puts serious areas of strength for an on reasonable asset the board. Customary practices frequently include repeating and regenerative ways to deal with agribusiness, ranger service, and fisheries.

By adjusting human exercises to normal cycles, native networks have supported biological systems for a really long time without draining assets or causing long haul ecological debasement.

Variation to Ecological Changes:

Native people group, frequently dwelling in naturally assorted and dynamic conditions, have versatile techniques to adapt to changing climatic circumstances. Customary information incorporates experiences into weather conditions, relocation courses, and occasional varieties, considering the variation of asset use examples to natural changes.

2. **Exceptional Viewpoints Presented by Native Information**
Intergenerational Shrewdness:

Native information is communicated through ages, encouraging a unique vault of shrewdness. Elderly folks inside native networks make light of a pivotal job in passing information about biological systems, asset the board, and social practices. This intergenerational move guarantees the progression and pertinence of customary biological information.

Social and Profound Associations:

Native information is profoundly interwoven with social and otherworldly convictions. The connection between native networks and the land is frequently consecrated, underlining an otherworldly association with nature. This otherworldly aspect encourages a feeling of obligation and stewardship, building up the inborn connection between social safeguarding and ecological preservation.

Place-Based Insight:

Native information is intrinsically nearby and place-based. It is customized to explicit biological systems, mirroring a significant comprehension of the one of a kind qualities of every climate. This restricted insight is urgent for making preservation procedures that are logically important and adjusted to the particular necessities of specific scenes.

Observational Learning:

Native information is fundamentally obtained through sharp perception and direct insight. This observational learning includes a profound association with the regular world, where local area individuals gain from the land, plants, and creatures. This experiential information is important for figuring out unpretentious natural changes and answering fittingly.

3. **Incorporating Native Information into Protection Systems**

Cooperative Direction:

Preservation drives benefit from consolidating native networks in dynamic cycles. Perceiving the worth of customary information and including native delegates in the preparation and execution of protection methodologies encourages a feeling of responsibility and guarantees that mediations line up with nearby real factors.

Local area Based Normal Asset The executives:

Embracing people group based normal asset the board (CBNRM) models that draw on native information upgrades protection results. This includes enabling neighborhood networks to oversee and safeguard their normal assets, utilizing customary practices to reasonably utilize and preserve biodiversity.

Social Planning and Customary Biological Information (TEK):

Social planning, an interaction that records native regions, social locales, and natural information, is an important instrument for protection arranging. Coordinating conventional environmental information (TEK) into planning endeavors gives a far reaching comprehension of biological systems and recognizes areas of natural importance.

Regarding Conventional Protection Practices:

Preservation endeavors ought to regard and support customary protection rehearses currently set up inside native networks. Whether it's rotational agribusiness, controlled consuming, or local area based preservation holds, perceiving and supporting these practices fortifies the texture of feasible asset the board.

Comprehensive Exploration Joint efforts:

Research coordinated efforts that span native information and logical request offer a strong road for upgrading protection understanding. These coordinated efforts perceive the corresponding idea of native and logical information frameworks, adding to more all encompassing and socially delicate preservation results.

4. **Challenges in Coordinating Native Information into Preservation**

Underestimation and Uprooting:

Native people group frequently face underestimation and uprooting, restricting their capacity to rehearse conventional land the board. Preservation endeavors need to address authentic shameful acts and engage native networks to hold and resuscitate their customary biological information.

Absence of Acknowledgment:

Native information is once in a while underestimated or excused in standard protection talk. Recognizing and esteeming the commitments of native information requires a change in perspective in protection practices and strategies.

Social Allotment:

The joining of native information into protection endeavors should be drawn nearer with aversion to stay away from social allotment. Joint efforts ought to focus on conscious commitment, with networks having office in how their insight is utilized and shared.

Language Boundaries:

Numerous native information frameworks are sent through oral practices in local dialects. Language obstructions can block viable correspondence among analysts and native networks. Drives ought to focus on interpretation and understanding to work with significant discourse.

5.3 Building Climate-Resilient Communities

Notwithstanding heightening environmental change influences, the basic to build environment strong networks has never been more dire. Environment flexibility includes improving the limit of networks to expect, answer, and recuperate from the antagonistic impacts of environmental change. This multi-layered approach coordinates versatile techniques, local area strengthening, and maintainable improvement rehearses.

Environment tough networks focus on different measures, for example, vigorous framework that can endure outrageous climate occasions, early admonition frameworks for catastrophic events, and supportable land-use arranging that thinks about environment changeability. Furthermore, people group commitment assumes an essential part, cultivating a feeling of pride and shared liability. Training and mindfulness drives enable inhabitants to go with informed choices, adjust to changing environment conditions, and add to decreasing their aggregate carbon impression.

By cultivating a culture of development, inclusivity, and joint effort, environment strong networks relieve the effects of environmental change as well as establish the groundwork for supportable, versatile, and flourishing social orders. In this aggregate undertaking, the objective isn't just to face the hardships of the present yet to fabricate networks that stand versatile against the vulnerabilities of a quickly changing environment in the years to come.

Chapter 6

Technological Innovations In Ecosystem Conservation

The crossing point of innovation and biological system protection has introduced another time of potential outcomes, offering inventive answers for address natural difficulties. Despite biodiversity misfortune, environmental change, and living space debasement, mechanical headways give apparatuses and systems to screen, dissect, and preserve environments all the more actually. This investigation digs into the assorted exhibit of mechanical advancements molding biological system preservation, going from remote detecting and man-made consciousness to resident science drives and state of the art observing gadgets.

1. **Remote Detecting and Earth Perception Advances**
   Satellite Symbolism and Observing:
   Satellite-based remote detecting has reformed our capacity to screen huge scope natural changes. High-goal satellite symbolism empowers researchers to follow deforestation, environment misfortune, and changes in land cover after some time. Constant checking recognizes basic regions for protection mediation and evaluate the effect of human exercises on biological systems.

Automated Ethereal Vehicles (UAVs) or Robots:

UAVs offer a flexible and financially savvy method for gathering point by point spatial information. Robots can be utilized for planning biodiversity, reviewing hard-to-arrive at regions, and checking natural life populaces. Their capacity to catch high-goal symbolism works with exact environment evaluations and supports preservation endeavors, especially in regions with testing territory.

Geographic Data Frameworks (GIS):

GIS innovation coordinates spatial information to make itemized maps, supporting environment examination and independent direction. Preservation experts use GIS to distinguish need regions for security, plan natural life hallways, and evaluate the availability of divided scenes. GIS assumes an essential part in enhancing asset designation for preservation projects.

2. **Man-made consciousness (simulated intelligence) and AI Species Distinguishing proof and Observing:**

Computer based intelligence controlled picture acknowledgment frameworks smooth out the recognizable proof of plant and creature species. AI calculations, prepared on tremendous datasets of species pictures, can quickly dissect field photos, adding to effective biodiversity observing. This innovation works with huge scope species inventories and helps track changes in populace elements.

Prescient Demonstrating for Protection Arranging:

AI calculations succeed at handling huge datasets to distinguish examples and patterns. In preservation arranging, these models can anticipate species circulation, survey natural surroundings appropriateness, and gauge the effect of environmental change on biological systems. Prescient demonstrating illuminates proactive preservation techniques by expecting future difficulties.

Computerized Preservation Checking Organizations:

Computer based intelligence driven checking networks mechanize the assortment and investigation of ecological information. These organizations can incorporate sensor frameworks, camera traps, and acoustic observing gadgets. By persistently handling information, computer based intelligence distinguishes inconsistencies or patterns that require consideration, empowering constant preservation the executives and reaction.

3. **Resident Science and Publicly supporting**
   Versatile Applications for Biodiversity Checking:
   Resident science drives influence versatile applications to connect with people in general in information assortment. Applications like iNaturalist permit clients to archive and share perceptions of plants and creatures, adding to enormous scope biodiversity data sets. Resident created information improves how we might interpret species circulations and supports preservation research.
   Publicly supported Ecological Information:
   Publicly supporting stages empower the assortment of ecological information from a different scope of sources. Projects like eBird for bird observing or OpenStreetMap for planning biological systems depend on commitments from people around the world. The aggregate force of publicly supported information upgrades the precision and inclusion of preservation data.

4. **High level Checking Gadgets and Sensors**
   Bioacoustic Checking Gadgets:
   Bioacoustic gadgets record sounds in common habitats, helping with the checking of untamed life and environments. These gadgets can distinguish species in light of their vocalizations, offering a non-meddlesome strategy for following biodiversity. Bioacoustics add to preservation endeavors by surveying environment wellbeing and distinguishing changes in species organization.
   Sensor Organizations for Environment and Natural Checking:
   Sending sensor networks considers continuous checking of ecological factors like temperature, stickiness, and air quality. These

organizations give persistent information streams, supporting the recognition of ecological changes and the evaluation of environment versatility. The Web of Things (IoT) works with the making of interconnected sensor networks for thorough checking.

5. **Preservation Hereditary qualities and DNA Innovations Natural DNA (eDNA) Examination:**

eDNA examination includes extricating hereditary material from natural examples like water or soil to distinguish the presence of species. This painless method is especially valuable for recognizing interesting or tricky species and evaluating the biodiversity of oceanic biological systems. eDNA adds to more productive and designated preservation endeavors.

Genomic Approaches for Protection:

Propels in genomics offer experiences into the hereditary variety and versatility of populaces. Protection hereditary procedures assist with surveying the wellbeing of populaces, recognize hereditarily unmistakable gatherings, and illuminate rearing projects for imperiled species. Genomic information improve the accuracy of preservation methodologies, guaranteeing they are custom fitted to the interesting hereditary cosmetics of target species.

6. **Blockchain Innovation for Protection**

Straightforward Store network The executives:

Blockchain innovation can be utilized to follow the beginning and inventory network of normal assets, like wood or fish. By giving a straightforward and alter safe record, blockchain helps battle unlawful logging and overfishing, advancing reasonable and moral practices.

Tokenized Preservation Motivating forces:

Blockchain-based frameworks empower the making of computerized tokens that address protection impetuses. These tokens can be given for confirmed ecological activities, like reforestation endeavors or untamed life assurance. Carrying out tokenized impetuses gives an original way to deal with preparing assets for protection projects.

7. Challenges and Moral Contemplations

Information Protection and Security:

The assortment and capacity of huge datasets, particularly those including touchy data, for example, species areas or native information, raise worries about information protection and security. Powerful moral systems are fundamental for address these issues and guarantee dependable information the executives.

Value in Innovation Access:

Differences in admittance to innovation, both among nations and inside networks, present difficulties to the impartial utilization of preservation advancements. Endeavors ought to be made to connect these holes, guaranteeing that the advantages of mechanical developments are shared internationally.

Algorithmic Predisposition and Decency:

AI calculations might display predisposition in view of the information they are prepared on, possibly prompting out of line results, especially in protection choices. Tending to algorithmic predisposition requires continuous checking, straightforwardness, and the joining of different viewpoints in the advancement cycle.

Local area Commitment and Strengthening:

While innovation offers useful assets for protection, the significant commitment of neighborhood networks is fundamental. Moral contemplations incorporate guaranteeing that innovation benefits, as opposed to dislodges, neighborhood information and practices. Engaging people group in the utilization of innovation encourages a cooperative way to deal with preservation.

6.1 Remote Sensing and Monitoring Tools

In the domain of biological system protection, the appearance of remote detecting and checking devices has changed our capacity to notice, break down, and oversee regular habitats. These innovations, going from satellite-based frameworks to ground-level sensors, give an abundance of information fundamental for grasping biological system elements, observing biodiversity, and executing viable protection methodologies.

This investigation digs into the assorted exhibit of remote detecting and checking devices, looking at their applications, advantages, and difficulties with regards to biological system protection.

1. **Satellite-Based Remote Detecting**

   Satellite Symbolism and Its Applications:

   Satellite-based remote detecting includes the utilization of Earth-noticing satellites outfitted with different sensors to catch symbolism and information. High-goal satellite symbolism is priceless for checking land cover changes, deforestation, and living space fracture. It gives a thorough perspective on enormous geographic regions, working with scene level evaluations.

   Vegetation Checking and Wellbeing Evaluation:

   Remote detecting satellites furnished with multispectral and hyperspectral sensors empower the observing of vegetation wellbeing. These sensors recognize various frequencies of light reflected by plants, permitting researchers to evaluate factors, for example, chlorophyll content, feelings of anxiety, and generally vegetation conditions. Such bits of knowledge are urgent for surveying biological system wellbeing and recognizing regions in danger.

   Land Use and Land Cover Planning:

   Satellite symbolism supports exact land use and land cover planning, fundamental for preservation arranging. By arranging different land cover types, including woods, wetlands, and metropolitan regions, scientists can assess changes after some time and recognize regions requiring assurance or rebuilding. This data guides land the executives choices and forestalls living space misfortune.

Environment Checking and Change Location:

Satellites add to environment checking by catching information on air conditions, ocean surface temperatures, and changes in ice cover. These perceptions are instrumental in understanding environment designs, recognizing shifts after some time, and evaluating the effect of environmental change on biological systems. Satellite information give a far reaching point of view on worldwide environment elements.

2. **Automated Flying Vehicles (UAVs) or Robots**

Accuracy Planning and Checking:

Automated Elevated Vehicles (UAVs), usually known as robots, offer an adaptable and savvy method for catching high-goal symbolism and information.

Drones are especially helpful for accuracy planning of more modest regions, for example, biodiversity areas of interest or rebuilding locales. Their dexterity takes into consideration definite appraisals of vegetation construction, geography, and natural surroundings qualities.

Untamed life Observing and Overviews:

Drones assume an essential part in untamed life checking, particularly in testing landscapes or distant areas. Outfitted with cameras and sensors, robots can direct aeronautical studies to appraise populace sizes, track creature developments, and screen settling destinations. This innovation limits aggravation to natural life and upgrades the effectiveness of biodiversity appraisals.

Quick Reaction to Natural Occasions:

Drones work with quick reaction to ecological occasions like fierce blazes, unlawful logging, or catastrophic events. They give continuous situational mindfulness, helping protectionists, and experts in settling on informed choices. Drones furnished with warm imaging might recognize heat oddities, distinguishing and battle woods fires early.

3. **Geographic Data Frameworks (GIS)**
Spatial Investigation and Direction:
Geographic Data Frameworks (GIS) coordinate spatial information to make layered maps, empowering modern spatial investigation. Protection professionals use GIS to survey the spatial connections between various biological elements, like the nearness of territories, network of scenes, and the conveyance of imperiled species. GIS illuminates dynamic cycles for powerful protection arranging.

Environment Network and Passage Arranging:
GIS innovation assumes a urgent part in surveying territory network and arranging untamed life passages. By investigating scene includes and recognizing likely boundaries to species development, GIS helps plan passages that upgrade biodiversity availability. This is especially significant for species movement, hereditary variety, and generally speaking biological system flexibility.

Biodiversity Area of interest ID:
GIS apparatuses help in distinguishing biodiversity areas of interest — regions with astoundingly high species extravagance and endemism. By overlaying layers of data on species appropriation, territory types, and environmental factors, GIS helps pinpoint districts of natural importance. This data guides protection needs and asset distribution.

4. **Man-made reasoning (simulated intelligence) and AI**
Robotized Species Recognizable proof:
Man-made intelligence and AI calculations are progressively utilized for the robotized recognizable proof of plant and creature species in huge datasets. Picture acknowledgment frameworks prepared on huge species data sets can break down photos and recognize species quickly. This innovation speeds up biodiversity observing endeavors and works with the production of extensive species inventories.

Prescient Displaying for Protection:

AI models succeed in handling immense datasets to distinguish designs and anticipate future patterns. In protection, these models are applied to anticipate species dispersion, evaluate environment reasonableness, and gauge the effect of environmental change on biological systems. Prescient displaying illuminates proactive protection systems by expecting possible difficulties.

Robotized Identification of Ecological Changes:

Man-made intelligence driven calculations can computerize the discovery of natural changes from satellite or robot symbolism. Whether it's distinguishing deforestation, following changes in water bodies, or identifying obtrusive species, AI calculations improve the effectiveness of observing endeavors. Constant discovery takes into consideration brief preservation intercessions.

5. **Challenges in Remote Detecting and Observing**

Information Availability and Expenses:

High-goal satellite symbolism and trend setting innovations can be exorbitant, restricting access for specialists and protection professionals, particularly in creating districts. Adjusting the requirement for point by point information with cost contemplations stays a test in guaranteeing broad utilization of remote detecting advances.

Information Handling and Understanding:

The sheer volume of information produced by remote detecting advances presents difficulties in handling and deciphering data. High level abilities in information examination and translation are required, featuring the significance of limit building and preparing for preservation experts.

Goal Impediments:

While satellite symbolism gives an expansive perspective on scenes, the goal may not be adequate for point by point evaluations, particularly in more modest protection regions. Finding some kind of harmony between the size of perception and the degree of detail expected for compelling protection stays a thought.

Moral Contemplations and Security:

The utilization of remote detecting advancements raises moral worries connected with security, especially while observing human exercises. Finding some kind of harmony between viable preservation checking and regarding protection privileges is vital, particularly in regions where neighborhood networks are involved.

6. Future Headings and Advancements

Reconciliation of Numerous Advancements:

The fate of remote detecting and checking lies in the reconciliation of numerous advancements. Consolidating satellite symbolism, drone-based information, ground-level sensors, and man-made intelligence driven investigation can give a more exhaustive comprehension of biological systems. This all encompassing methodology improves the exactness and significance of preservation evaluations.

Headways in Sensor Advancements:

Progressing headways in sensor advancements, remembering upgrades for goal, otherworldly abilities, and scaling down, will add to additional definite and exact information assortment. These headways empower analysts to screen environments at better scales, catching subtleties that were beforehand unavailable.

Resident Science and Remote Detecting Collaborations:

Coordinating resident science drives with remote detecting innovations offers a synergistic way to deal with information assortment. Resident researchers can contribute ground-level perceptions that supplement satellite or robot information. This cooperative methodology upgrades information exactness and connects with nearby networks in protection endeavors.

Open Information Stages and Joint effort:

Open information stages and cooperative drives work with the sharing of remote detecting information and devices. By advancing openness and joint effort, these stages add to a more comprehensive and worldwide way to deal with biological system preservation. Open information drives support straightforwardness and energize the cooperation of assorted partners.

6.2 Climate Modeling for Conservation Planning

Environmental change presents remarkable difficulties to worldwide biological systems, impacting temperature designs, precipitation systems, and the recurrence of outrageous climate occasions. Despite these changes, preservation arranging has developed to integrate environment displaying as an essential instrument.

Environment models reenact future environment situations, assisting protectionists with expecting the effect of environmental change on biological systems and species. This investigation digs into the meaning of environment demonstrating in preservation arranging, analyzing its applications, philosophies, and the crucial job it plays in advancing biological system flexibility.

1. **Understanding Environment Displaying**
   Definition and Reason:
   Environment displaying includes the utilization of numerical portrayals to reenact Earth's environment framework. These models think about different variables, including barometrical circumstances, sea flows, and land surface cooperations. The main role of environment demonstrating in preservation arranging is to project future climatic circumstances, permitting researchers and protectionists to survey how biological systems might answer changing ecological boundaries.
   Sorts of Environment Models:
   Environment models can be extensively classified into worldwide environment models (GCMs) and provincial environment models (RCMs). GCMs give a wide outline of environment designs at a worldwide scale, while RCMs offer more point by point data at territorial or nearby levels. The two kinds of models contribute

important experiences to preservation arranging by recreating various parts of environment elements.

2. **Uses of Environment Demonstrating in Protection**

Surveying Species Weakness:

Environment models assist with surveying the weakness of species to environmental change by projecting how their territories might move over the long haul. This data is basic for recognizing in danger species and focusing on preservation endeavors in regions where living spaces are supposed to go through huge changes.

Natural surroundings Reasonableness Demonstrating:

Natural surroundings reasonableness models incorporate environment information with biological inclinations of species to foresee the future dispersion of appropriate territories. These models help with distinguishing regions where species are probably going to flourish under changing environment conditions. Preservation organizers utilize this data to configuration safeguarded regions and plan natural surroundings rebuilding projects.

Distinguishing Environment Refugia:

Environment refugia are regions that remain moderately steady and give shelter to species during times of environmental change. Environment models help recognize these refugia, permitting traditionalists to focus on security and the board endeavors in regions that might act as shelters for biodiversity.

Passage Plan for Species Development:

Environment models add to planning natural life passageways by anticipating how scenes might change over the long haul. These halls associate divided territories, working with the development of species in light of environment driven shifts. Guaranteeing network is significant for keeping up with hereditary variety and supporting species transformation.

3. **Philosophies in Environment Demonstrating for Protection Paleoclimate Information Coordination:**

Environment models frequently consolidate paleoclimate information, which gives bits of knowledge into past environment varieties. By dissecting verifiable environment designs, researchers can work on the precision of future environment projections. Paleoclimate information additionally recognizes normal environment fluctuation, recognizing it from anthropogenic impacts.

Downscaling Procedures:

GCMs, with their worldwide scale center, may miss the mark on goal required for provincial or nearby protection arranging. Downscaling methods overcome this issue by refining worldwide environment projections to give higher-goal data at local scales. RCMs and factual downscaling strategies improve the accuracy of environment displaying for confined appraisals.

Gathering Demonstrating:

Gathering demonstrating includes running different reenactments with varieties in model boundaries or beginning circumstances. This approach helps catch the scope of vulnerabilities inborn in environment demonstrating. Protection organizers use group models to all the more likely comprehend the scope of conceivable future environment situations, empowering more powerful independent direction.

Consolidating Biophysical Inputs:

Environment models progressively consolidate biophysical criticisms, taking into account how changes in environment impact natural cycles as well as the other way around.

For instance, modifications in vegetation examples might influence nearby environment conditions. By incorporating these inputs, models give a more sensible portrayal of the complicated connections among environment and biological systems.

4. **Difficulties and Vulnerabilities in Environment Displaying for Protection**

Vulnerabilities in Emanation Situations:

Future environment projections rely upon situations of ozone harming substance emanations. Different emanation situations lead to shifting environment results, presenting vulnerabilities in displaying. The development of human exercises and strategies decides emanation directions, making it trying to foresee with conviction.

Intricacy of Biological system Reactions:

Biological system reactions to environmental change are intricate and diverse. Environment models frequently work on these connections, prompting vulnerabilities in anticipating how species and biological systems will adjust. The unique idea of biological cycles presents difficulties in precisely addressing biodiversity reactions.

Impediments in Spatial and Fleeting Goal:

Worldwide environment models might miss the mark on spatial and fleeting goal required for fine-scale preservation arranging. Depending entirely on GCMs might bring about disregarding nearby varieties that are pivotal for figuring out species elements. Downscaling strategies address this limit, yet challenges in accomplishing high accuracy persevere.

Non-Environment Stressors:

Environment models may not completely represent non-environment stressors, like territory debasement, contamination, or obtrusive species. These stressors can fuel the effect of environmental change on biological systems. Incorporated demonstrating approaches that think about both environment and non-environment stressors give a more thorough premise to protection arranging.

5. **Versatile Administration Methodologies Informed by Environment Demonstrating**

Adaptable Protection Plans:

Versatile administration includes adaptable protection designs that can be changed in light of new data or evolving conditions. Environment demonstrating illuminates versatile administration by giving a premise to expecting possible changes in biological systems. Preservation procedures can be intended to oblige developing environment situations.

Dynamic Safeguarded Region Organizations:

Environment demonstrating guides the plan of dynamic safeguarded region networks that record for moving natural surroundings. As opposed to static limits, safeguarded regions can be planned with adaptability, considering changes in light of environment driven changes in species conveyances. This approach upgrades the viability of protection endeavors.

Focusing on Tough Biological systems:

Tough biological systems, distinguished through environment displaying, can be focused on for preservation intercessions. These biological systems might have the ability to endure and recuperate from environment related unsettling influences. Zeroing in endeavors on strong regions adds to the general versatility and flexibility of the protection scene.

6. **Reconciliation with Preservation Strategy and Independent direction**

Integrating Environment Models into Regulation:

Preservation strategies can profit from integrating environment models into authoritative systems. This coordination guarantees that environment contemplations are integral to protection arranging and that strategies line up with the extended effects of environmental change on biodiversity.

Multi-Partner Commitment:

Environment models give a shared belief to multi-partner commitment in preservation arranging. By introducing experimentally educated projections, models work with cooperative independent direction including government organizations, NGOs, neighborhood networks, and examination foundations. This comprehensive methodology improves the execution of powerful protection measures.

Limit Working for Chiefs:

Compelling utilization of environment models in preservation arranging requires limit working for chiefs. Preparing projects and studios can enable protection specialists, policymakers, and nearby networks to comprehend, decipher, and apply environment model results in their dynamic cycles.

6.3 Citizen Science and Data Collection

Resident science, a cooperative way to deal with logical exploration including the support of general society, has arisen as an amazing asset for information assortment in the domain of ecological protection. Connecting with residents in logical undertakings cultivates a feeling of aggregate liability, improves public mindfulness, and produces immense datasets that add to how we might interpret environments.

This investigation digs into the meaning of resident science in information assortment for natural protection, analyzing its advantages, philosophies, and the extraordinary effect it has on logical exploration.

1. **The Pith of Resident Science**

   Characterizing Resident Science:

   Resident science includes the dynamic association of non-proficient workers, frequently people from the overall population, in logical examination projects. These ventures length different logical disciplines, including environment, cosmology, and biodiversity checking. With regards to ecological preservation, resident science assumes a significant part in information assortment, empowering scientists to accumulate data on a scale and degree that sounds in any case testing, truly.

   Various Investment:

   Resident science drives draw in members from assorted foundations, ages, and mastery levels. This inclusivity improves the wealth of information by integrating perceptions according to different points of view. From younger students taking part in bird builds up to retired folks checking water quality, resident science projects influence the energy and interest of people with a scope of encounters.

2. **Advantages of Resident Science in Ecological Information Assortment**

Expanded Spatial and Worldly Inclusion:

Resident science fundamentally extends the spatial and fleeting inclusion of information assortment endeavors. Customary exploration strategies might be restricted by asset limitations, however resident researchers can contribute information across expansive geographic regions and overstretched periods. This far reaching inclusion is especially significant for observing enormous biological systems or following occasional changes.

Practical Information Assortment:

Utilizing the force of workers decreases the expense of information assortment. Conventional logical examination frequently requires significant subsidizing for hardware, faculty, and coordinated factors. Resident science projects gain by the eagerness of workers to contribute their time and exertion, empowering analysts to accomplish aggressive information assortment objectives with additional unassuming financial plans.

Improved Public Commitment and Mindfulness:

Resident science encourages public commitment to logical undertakings, advancing ecological mindfulness and instruction. By including residents in information assortment, people gain a more profound comprehension of nearby biological systems and the logical cycle. This expanded mindfulness can prompt more educated natural direction and a more noteworthy feeling of ecological stewardship.

Local area Strengthening:

Resident science enables networks to take part in the protection of their neighborhood surroundings effectively. At the point when residents add to information assortment endeavors, they become partners in the logical cycle, building up a feeling of pride and obligation. This strengthening can prompt local area driven preservation drives and a more grounded association among individuals and their normal environmental factors.

3. **Strategies in Resident Science Information Assortment**

Organic Checking:

Resident researchers frequently take part in organic observing, including bird watching, butterfly counts, and plant studies. These exercises contribute significant information on species appropriation, overflow, and phenology. Projects like the Christmas Bird Count and the Incomparable Lawn Bird Count include great many members around the world, giving basic data to avian protection.

Water Quality Observing:

Checking water quality is a typical focal point of resident science drives. Volunteers might gather tests from nearby water bodies, measure boundaries like pH and supplement levels, and report their discoveries. This information helps with the appraisal of water quality, distinguishing proof of contamination sources, and improvement of systems for water asset the executives.

Air Quality Checking:

Resident researchers can add to air quality checking by utilizing minimal expense sensors to quantify contaminations like particulate matter and nitrogen dioxide. These endeavors give restricted information on air quality, assisting analysts and policymakers with tending to ecological wellbeing concerns. Drives, for example, "resident air quality observing organizations" exhibit the capability of resident science in this area.

Biodiversity Perceptions through Innovation:

Innovation, including cell phones and committed applications, works with the assortment of biodiversity perceptions. Stages like iNaturalist permit clients to report and share their perceptions of plants, creatures, and parasites.

AI calculations can aid species distinguishing proof, making a tremendous information base of biodiversity records contributed by resident researchers universally.

4. **Difficulties and Contemplations in Resident Science Information Assortment**

Information Quality and Normalization:

Guaranteeing the quality and normalization of information gathered by resident researchers is a pivotal test. Changing degrees of skill among members might prompt irregularities. Carrying out preparing programs, laying out clear conventions, and integrating approval cycles can improve the dependability of resident science information.

Information Inclination and Spatial Representativeness:

Resident science information might show inclinations, as specific geographic regions or biological systems might be overrepresented or underrepresented. Tending to spatial inclinations requires designated enrollment endeavors and key venture plan to guarantee an all the more even dissemination of information across locales and biological systems.

Keeping up with Member Commitment:

Supporting member commitment over the long haul is a typical test in resident science projects. Rousing workers and keeping them included requires successful correspondence, acknowledgment of commitments, and the production of a steady local area. Consolidating gamification components or giving substantial advantages, like instructive assets, can assist with keeping up with interest.

Moral Contemplations:

Moral contemplations, including the dependable treatment of information, guaranteeing member security, and acquiring informed assent, are principal in resident science. Analysts should lay out clear moral rules and conventions to protect the privileges and prosperity of members.

5. **Incorporating Resident Science into Protection Arrangements and Independent direction**

Strategy Acknowledgment and Backing:

Perceiving the worth of resident science, policymakers can incorporate resident produced information into ecological independent direction. This acknowledgment might include creating structures that recognize the believability of resident science information and integrating it into true observing and detailing components.

Coordinated effort with Government Organizations:

Cooperation between resident science tasks and government organizations upgrades the effect of information gathered by volunteers. Government offices can profit from the extra information sources given by resident researchers, prompting more far reaching and informed protection approaches. The incorporation of resident science information might add to the versatile administration of normal assets.

Consideration in Ecological Effect Evaluations:

Resident science information can be integrated into ecological effect evaluations (EIAs) to give a more comprehensive comprehension of biological system wellbeing. Consideration in EIAs guarantees that local area points of view and privately assembled information add to the assessment of likely ecological effects, upgrading the general precision and viability of appraisals.

Chapter 7

Challenges And Barriers To Effective Conservation

Preservation, the security and feasible administration of Earth's biodiversity, is a basic endeavor notwithstanding raising ecological difficulties. While the objective of protection is clear — to keep up with the wellbeing and variety of biological systems — accomplishing this goal is loaded with intricacies. This investigation dives into the bunch difficulties and hindrances that upset successful protection endeavors. From anthropogenic exercises and natural surroundings corruption to financial elements and institutional constraints, understanding these difficulties is fundamental for planning systems that can address the underlying drivers of biodiversity misfortune and advance long haul biological manageability.

1. **Anthropogenic Tensions on Environments**
   Living space Annihilation and Discontinuity:
   One of the first difficulties to successful preservation is living space annihilation and fracture. Urbanization, farming extension, and foundation advancement lead to the adjustment and discontinuity of normal living spaces. This interaction segregates

populaces, disturbs natural cycles, and decreases the general versatility of biological systems.

Deforestation and Land Use Change:

Deforestation, driven by logging, farming, and land transformation, represents a huge danger to biodiversity. The deficiency of timberlands brings about the obliteration of living spaces for endless species, prompting decreases in populaces and adding to the disturbance of environmental equilibrium.

Environmental Change and An Earth-wide temperature boost:

Environmental change is an unavoidable test that influences biodiversity on a worldwide scale. Increasing temperatures, changing precipitation examples, and outrageous climate occasions straightforwardly influence biological systems and species. Changes in environment conditions adjust the conveyance of species, influencing their overflow and endurance.

Contamination and Defilement:

Contamination from different sources, including modern releases, farming overflow, and plastic waste, represents a serious danger to biological systems. Foreign substances in air, water, and soil adversely influence natural life, upset pecking orders, and add to the decay of weak species.

2. **Overexploitation of Normal Assets**

Overharvesting and Abuse:

Overexploitation of normal assets, for example, overfishing, unlawful logging, and poaching, undermines numerous species with elimination. Impractical reaping practices can drain populaces, disturb biological systems, and lead to flowing environmental results.

Obtrusive Species:

The presentation of non-local species into new biological systems can devastatingly affect neighborhood biodiversity. Intrusive species frequently outcompete local widely varied vegetation, prompting the decay or annihilation of native species. The spread of intrusive species is worked with by worldwide exchange and human exercises.

3. **Financial Variables**

Populace Development and Urbanization:

Human populace development and urbanization apply huge strain on normal assets. As populaces grow and metropolitan regions spread, the interest for land, water, and energy increments, frequently to the detriment of biodiversity-rich environments.

Neediness and Asset Reliance:

Neediness and a reliance on normal assets for livelihoods add to unreasonable practices. Networks confronting monetary difficulties might fall back on exercises like unlawful logging, overfishing, or impractical horticulture, compounding the debasement of biological systems.

Absence of Monetary Motivations for Preservation:

By and large, financial motivators leaning toward asset double-dealing over protection endeavors block biodiversity safeguarding. The momentary financial increases related with exercises like logging or mining might offset the drawn out advantages of preservation, prompting an absence of inspiration for economical practices.

4. **Institutional and Strategy Difficulties**

Lacking Legitimate Systems:

Feeble or deficient legitimate systems for preservation add to the difficulties looked in saving biodiversity. In certain locales, remiss requirement of ecological regulations and guidelines permits disastrous practices to proceed unabated.

Unfortunate Administration and Defilement:

Unfortunate administration, defilement, and absence of straightforwardness in normal asset the executives worsen preservation challenges. While dynamic cycles are defaced by debasement, reserves expected for protection might be abused, and authorization of guidelines might be compromised.

Absence of Coordinated Arranging:

Protection endeavors are in many cases upset by an absence of co-ordinated arranging that considers both natural and financial elements. Divided arranging can prompt clashing area use choices, hampering the adequacy of protection systems.

5. **Logical and Information Holes**

Lacking Information and Checking:

Preservation endeavors depend intensely on precise information and observing, yet numerous districts need adequate data on the situation with biodiversity. Lacking gauge information and observing frameworks make it trying to survey the viability of protection intercessions and answer arising dangers.

Restricted Comprehension of Environment Elements:

Environments are many-sided and interconnected frameworks, and holes in how we might interpret their elements frustrate powerful protection. Restricted information on species cooper-ations, natural cycles, and the drawn out effects of human exer-cises obstructs the plan of focused on and fruitful protection techniques.

6. **Human-Untamed life Struggle**

Loss of Territory and Infringement:

As human populaces grow, clashes among people and natural life become more common. Loss of territory powers natural life into closer vicinity to human settlements, prompting episodes of yield striking, property harm, and human-natural life conflicts.

Negative Discernments and Retaliatory Killings:

Pessimistic impression of natural life, frequently filled by finan-cial misfortunes or worries for individual wellbeing, can bring about retaliatory killings of creatures. This represents an immedi-ate danger to numerous species, particularly huge carnivores and hunters.

7. **Environmental Change Vulnerabilities**
Vulnerabilities in Environment Demonstrating:
While environmental change is a deeply grounded danger, vulnerabilities in environment models and expectations make it trying to expect its nearby and provincial effects definitively. This vulnerability muddles preservation arranging and variation systems.

Changes in Species Circulations:
Environmental change-actuated shifts in species appropriations present difficulties for preservation endeavors. Species might move to new regions in light of evolving environments, possibly prompting the making of novel biological systems and requiring versatile administration methodologies.

8. **Public Mindfulness and Commitment**
Restricted Public Mindfulness:
Deficient public mindfulness and comprehension of biodiversity issues prevent protection endeavors. An absence of mindfulness can bring about unresponsiveness or detachment, diminishing help for protection drives and making it hard to prepare public activity.

Correspondence Holes:
Successfully imparting complex logical data to general society is a persevering test. Overcoming any barrier between logical discoveries and public comprehension is essential for earning backing and encouraging an aggregate obligation to preservation.

9. **Social and Moral Contemplations**
Social Works on Influencing Protection:
Certain social practices might add to biodiversity misfortune. For instance, the utilization of customary restorative plants or chasing after social ceremonies can apply strain on imperiled species. Offsetting social legacy with preservation objectives requires cautious thought.

Moral Contemplations in Protection Systems:

Moral predicaments might emerge in protection systems, especially when mediations include compromises or possible contentions with nearby networks. Regarding the privileges and points of view of native people groups and neighborhood networks is fundamental for morally sound preservation rehearses.

10. **Protection Financing and Asset Allotment**

Restricted Financing for Protection:

Deficient monetary assets distributed to preservation projects limit the degree and size of drives. Preservation endeavors require critical financing for research, living space reclamation, against poaching measures, and local area commitment. Rivalry for restricted assets might bring about a few basic tasks being disregarded.

Inconsistent Asset Dissemination:

Asset dissemination is frequently inconsistent, for certain areas getting more consideration and financing than others. This unevenness might disregard biodiversity-rich regions confronting serious dangers. Tending to this difference requires a more fair dispersion of assets in light of protection needs.

11. **Worldwide Coordination and Joint effort**

Divided Worldwide Protection Endeavors:

Regardless of the worldwide idea of biodiversity challenges, preservation endeavors are frequently divided and need durable coordination. The shortfall of a brought together methodology can bring about copied endeavors, failures, and holes in tending to cross-limit protection issues.

Political and Strategic Difficulties:

Preservation endeavors might be ruined by political and discretionary difficulties, particularly while tending to transboundary protection issues. Arranging arrangements, planning endeavors across borders, and exploring international intricacies require strategic artfulness.

7.1 Human-Induced Obstacles

As mankind propels innovatively, extends its impression, and changes normal scenes, the multifaceted dance between human exercises and biodiversity turns out to be progressively weighty. Human-prompted snags to preservation present critical difficulties, undermining the fragile equilibrium of environments and adding to the worldwide decay of biodiversity. This investigation digs into the diverse idea of human-instigated hindrances, going from direct double-dealing of assets to circuitous effects, for example, environmental change and contamination. Understanding these hindrances is vital for planning powerful procedures that moderate human effects and cultivate an agreeable concurrence among individuals and the normal world.

1. **Double-dealing of Regular Assets**
   Overharvesting and Unreasonable Extraction:
   The persistent quest for regular assets, driven by expanding requests for food, wood, and minerals, brings about overharvesting and impractical extraction rehearses. Overfishing, clear-cutting of woods, and mining exercises can drain populaces and corrupt living spaces, endangering the strength of environments.
   Unlawful Untamed life Exchange:
   The unlawful natural life exchange, driven by an interest for colorful pets, customary meds, and elaborate things, represents a serious danger to numerous species. Poaching for ivory, rhino horn, and extraordinary skins, among different items, adds to populace declines and disturbs environmental equilibrium.
   Modern Farming and Land Change:
   The extension of modern farming, combined with land change for urbanization, changes immense plots of normal environment into monoculture fields or created regions. This change pieces biological systems, dislodges natural life, and adds to the deficiency of biodiversity-rich scenes.
2. **Living space Obliteration and Discontinuity**
   Deforestation and Urbanization:

Deforestation, frequently determined by rural development and logging, prompts the annihilation of basic living spaces. Urbanization worsens this interaction, supplanting regular scenes with substantial designs and impenetrable surfaces, further dividing environments.

Framework Improvement and Discontinuity:

The development of streets, roadways, and dams can part environments and make obstructions to untamed life development. Divided scenes hinder species' capacity to relocate, track down food, and repeat, expanding their weakness to annihilation.

3. **Contamination and Tainting**

Synthetic Contamination:

Synthetic toxins from modern and rural exercises, including pesticides, manures, and modern effluents, defile air, water, and soil. These contaminations adversely affect biodiversity, prompting decreases in bug populaces, disturbances in amphibian environments, and long haul medical problems for untamed life.

Plastic Contamination:

The expansion of plastic contamination, driven by single-use plastics and ill-advised garbage removal, represents a danger to marine and earthbound environments. Natural life, including marine creatures and birds, ingest or become caught in plastic garbage, bringing about injury, suffocation, and passing.

Air and Commotion Contamination:

Air contamination, brought about by emanations from vehicles, modern offices, and power plants, adds to respiratory issues in natural life and influences plant wellbeing. Commotion contamination, frequently connected with metropolitan regions and transportation courses, disturbs creature correspondence, route, and regenerative ways of behaving.

4. **Environmental Change Effects**

Climbing Temperatures and Modified Environment Examples:

Human-actuated environmental change, basically determined by the ignition of petroleum derivatives and deforestation, prompts climbing worldwide temperatures and modified environment designs. These progressions influence biological systems by influencing the dispersion of species, adjusting precipitation systems, and affecting the recurrence and force of outrageous climate occasions.

Sea Fermentation:

The retention of overabundance carbon dioxide by the world's seas prompts sea fermentation, which represents a danger to marine life, especially living beings with calcium carbonate skeletons or shells. Coral reefs, specifically, are helpless against the impacts of fermentation, imperiling the whole marine environment they support.

Ocean Level Ascent:

Softening polar ice covers and glacial masses, an outcome of an Earth-wide temperature boost, add to rising ocean levels. This represents an immediate danger to seaside biological systems and the species that possess them, prompting territory misfortune, expanded saltiness, and disturbances in waterfront biodiversity.

5. **Intrusive Species and Biotic Homogenization**

Presentation of Non-Local Species:

Human exercises, including worldwide exchange and travel, acquaint non-local species with new biological systems. These obtrusive species can outcompete local verdure, disturb biological cycles, and add to the downfall of native biodiversity.

Biotic Homogenization:

The spread of obtrusive species, joined with the deficiency of local species, prompts biotic homogenization — the cycle by which biological systems become more comparable in species arrangement. This deficiency of biodiversity and the normalization of environments lessen the remarkable natural ascribes of various districts.

6. **Overpopulation and Utilization**
Populace Strain:
Human overpopulation puts massive tension on normal assets. As the worldwide populace keeps on developing, the interest for food, water, and land expands, prompting escalated double-dealing of biological systems and worsening the difficulties looked by preservation endeavors.
Industrialism and Asset Utilization:
Impractical utilization designs, driven by commercialization and the quest for monetary development, add to asset exhaustion and natural corruption. The extraction and handling of unrefined components for assembling and the removal of waste put an extra weight on biological systems.

7. **Moral and Social Contemplations**
Social Works on Affecting Biodiversity:
Certain social practices, like conventional medication or the utilization of creature parts in customs, can affect biodiversity. Off-setting social legacy with protection objectives requires nuanced approaches that regard social variety while advancing economical practices.
Moral Situations in Protection Systems:
Protection methodologies might confront moral predicaments, especially when mediations include compromises or possible contentions with neighborhood networks. Regarding the privileges and viewpoints of native people groups and nearby networks is fundamental for moral preservation rehearses.

8. **Absence of Ecological Training and Mindfulness**
Restricted Ecological Training:
An absence of far reaching ecological instruction adds to an absence of mindfulness with respect to biodiversity issues. Without understanding the interconnectedness of biological systems and the significance of biodiversity, people may accidentally take part in exercises that hurt the climate.

Disengage from Nature:

Urbanization and current ways of life frequently bring about a distinction from nature. This separation lessens the worth put on biodiversity and decreases the awareness of certain expectations for ecological stewardship.

9. **Institutional and Strategy Difficulties**

Insufficient Legitimate Systems and Authorization:

Frail or inadequate legitimate systems for protection, combined with remiss requirement of ecological regulations, add to human-actuated deterrents. In certain areas, administrative provisos and deficient punishments permit disastrous practices to continue.

Absence of Combination in Arranging:

An absence of incorporation between protection endeavors and more extensive improvement arranging hampers compelling biodiversity conservation. Preservation should be consistently coordinated into land-use arranging, foundation advancement, and financial strategies to guarantee maintainability.

10. **Worldwide Financial Variations**

Inconsistent Dispersion of Assets:

Worldwide financial variations add to natural corruption. Locales with restricted assets might focus on momentary financial additions over long haul preservation, compounding the difficulties looked by biodiversity-rich regions.

Absence of Worldwide Collaboration:

Lacking worldwide collaboration and coordination obstruct endeavors to address worldwide protection challenges. Transboundary issues, like transitory species and shared environments, require cooperative arrangements that are many times impeded by international intricacies.

7.2 Funding and Resource Limitations

Protection endeavors overall are faced by a basic and inescapable test — lacking financing and asset constraints. The complex undertaking of saving biodiversity needs monetary help for research, territory assurance, against poaching measures, and local area commitment. Notwithstanding, compelled financial plans, contending needs, and inconsistent asset dispersion frustrate the extension and effect of preservation drives. This investigation digs into the intricacies of subsidizing and asset limits in protection, analyzing the outcomes of lacking monetary help and proposing techniques to address these difficulties.

1. **Restricted Financing for Protection Drives**
   Asset Designation Inconsistencies:
   Protection endeavors frequently fight with variations in asset distribution. A few locales, especially those with high biodiversity and confronting serious dangers, may get deficient financing contrasted with regions with more noteworthy monetary impact. This lopsidedness sustains the weakness of biodiversity-rich areas.
   Contending Needs:
   States and associations face a bunch of contending needs, going from medical services and training to foundation improvement. Protection might be eclipsed by additional prompt and substantial worries, bringing about restricted monetary help for biodiversity conservation.
   Deficient Public and Confidential Financing:
   Public and confidential financing for protection might miss the mark concerning the assets expected to address the diverse difficulties confronting biodiversity. Deficient monetary support restricts the execution of extensive preservation techniques, ruining the capacity to safeguard and economically oversee biological systems.

2. **Results of Subsidizing and Asset Limits**
   Disabled Exploration and Observing:
   Lacking financing sabotages significant examination and checking exercises fundamental for figuring out environments and species elements. Lacking monetary help restricts the capacity to accumulate information, direct long haul studies, and screen the

effects of human exercises on biodiversity.

Diminished Limit with respect to Hostile to Poaching and Authorization:

The battle against unlawful natural life exchange and poaching requires significant assets for watches, reconnaissance, and policing. Restricted subsidizing compromises the ability to convey staff, utilize cutting edge innovations, and execute compelling techniques to battle natural life wrongdoing.

Natural surroundings Corruption and Misfortune:

Financing impediments add to living space debasement and misfortune, as preservation associations battle to get and oversee safeguarded regions. Without sufficient assets, environment reclamation and assurance endeavors are inadequate to moderate the effects of urbanization, deforestation, and land change.

Insufficient People group Commitment:

Successful preservation includes connecting with neighborhood networks in manageable practices and cultivating a feeling of stewardship. Restricted assets obstruct local area effort and training drives, thwarting the improvement of associations that are urgent for the progress of protection projects.

3. **Systems to Address Financing and Asset Impediments**

Broadening of Financing Sources:

Protection associations can alleviate financing difficulties by enhancing their wellsprings of help. Past government awards, associations with generous establishments, corporate supporters, and public-private joint efforts can upgrade monetary versatility and widen the extent of preservation drives.

Advancement of Practical Supporting Models:

Embracing practical supporting models, for example, eco-the travel industry, installment for environment administrations, and biodiversity balances, can produce income for preservation projects. These models coordinate monetary exercises with biodiversity protection, making a self-supporting pattern of financing.

Expanded Public Mindfulness and Backing:

Raising public mindfulness about the significance of biodiversity and earning support through backing endeavors can invigorate expanded financing. A very much educated public is bound to pressure legislatures, enterprises, and worldwide bodies to dispense assets to protection.

Vital Organizations and Cooperation:

Cooperative associations between states, non-legislative associations (NGOs), and confidential elements can pool assets, share skill, and all in all address financing limits. Multilateral coordinated efforts can use assorted points of view and wellsprings of help for more significant protection results.

Consolidation of Innovation for Cost-Effectiveness:

Embracing mechanical developments, like remote detecting, man-made brainpower, and information examination, can upgrade the productivity of protection endeavors. Innovation driven arrangements can smooth out information assortment, further develop checking capacities, and improve asset use.

Long haul Interest in Limit Building:

Putting resources into the limit working of nearby networks, protection associations, and legislative organizations makes an establishment for supported biodiversity safeguarding. Limit building incorporates preparing programs, ability advancement, and the foundation of neighborhood mastery, diminishing reliance on outer financing over the long run.

Promotion for Strategy Changes:

Protection associations can advocate for strategy changes that focus on biodiversity safeguarding. Drawing in with policymakers to lay out and reinforce regulation, authorize natural guidelines, and coordinate protection into public advancement plans can bring about expanded government financing and backing.

4. **Worldwide Cooperation and Subsidizing Drives**

Worldwide Subsidizing Systems:

Worldwide bodies and benefactor offices assume a urgent part in supporting worldwide protection drives. Drives like the Worldwide Climate Office (GEF), the Green Environment Asset (GCF), and the Show on Organic Variety (CBD) give roads to nations to get to subsidizing for biodiversity protection.

Corporate Social Obligation (CSR):

Empowering corporate substances to embrace natural manageability and add to preservation through CSR drives can be a critical wellspring of financing. Associations between preservation associations and organizations can adjust financial exercises to environmental obligation.

Obligation for-Nature Trades:

Obligation for-nature trades include rebuilding a country's obligation in return for responsibilities to put resources into preservation and manageable turn of events. This imaginative supporting component tends to both monetary difficulties and biodiversity safeguarding, giving a mutually beneficial answer for indebted person countries and the worldwide climate.

7.3 Balancing Conservation with Human Needs

The fragile transaction among protection and human requirements typifies one of the most intricate difficulties of the advanced period. As the worldwide populace proceeds to develop and human exercises apply expanding tension on regular biological systems, finding some kind of harmony between biodiversity safeguarding and addressing the requirements of human networks becomes fundamental.

This investigation dives into the complex elements of offsetting preservation with human requirements, inspecting the contending interests, moral contemplations, and creative procedures that support the quest for reasonable conjunction.

1. **Contending Interests: Biodiversity Safeguarding versus Human Turn of events**
   Land Use Clashes:

The distribution of land for preservation purposes frequently clashes with the interest for space for horticulture, urbanization, and framework improvement. Adjusting the requirement for safeguarded regions with the extending prerequisites of human social orders requires cautious preparation and discussion.

Asset Extraction and Abuse:

Human exercises like logging, mining, and fishing frequently crash into protection goals. The extraction of normal assets is fundamental for financial turn of events, however it represents a danger to environments and biodiversity. Alleviating these contentions requires economical asset the executives rehearses.

Horticultural Extension and Natural surroundings Misfortune:

The development of agribusiness to fulfill the developing need for food adds to living space misfortune and discontinuity. Adjusting the requirement for agrarian creation with environment safeguarding includes carrying out manageable cultivating works on, safeguarding basic regions, and advancing agroecological approaches.

2. **Moral Contemplations in Adjusting Protection and Human Necessities**

Freedoms of Native People groups and Neighborhood People group:

Numerous protection regions are occupied by native people groups and neighborhood networks whose livelihoods are complicatedly attached to the land. Regarding their freedoms, conventional information, and support in dynamic cycles are fundamental moral contemplations in protection endeavors.

Natural Equity:

Natural equity contemplations accentuate the evenhanded dispersion of the advantages and weights of preservation measures. Offsetting preservation with human necessities requires guaranteeing that underestimated networks don't bear unbalanced adverse consequences while profiting from protection drives.

Social Legacy Safeguarding:

Offsetting preservation endeavors with human requirements includes protecting social legacy interlaced with regular scenes. Conventional practices, otherworldly convictions, and social personalities frequently depend on the biological systems in which networks have flourished for ages.

3. **Creative Procedures for Practical Conjunction**

Local area Based Preservation:

Connecting with nearby networks in protection drives encourages a feeling of pride and shared liability. Local area based protection approaches enable individuals to take part in biodiversity safeguarding, adjusting preservation objectives to neighborhood requirements and yearnings effectively.

Installment for Biological system Administrations (PES):

Installment for Environment Administrations is an inventive methodology that perceives the worth of nature's administrations. By remunerating networks for keeping up with solid environments, PES adjusts preservation to human requirements, making monetary motivations for maintainable practices.

Agroforestry and Manageable Farming:

Advancing agroforestry and manageable agrarian practices incorporates biodiversity preservation with food creation. These methodologies improve biological system flexibility, safeguard biodiversity, and give maintainable livelihoods to networks reliant upon agribusiness.

Ecotourism:

Ecotourism addresses a practical financial elective that adjusts preservation to human requirements. By displaying regular magnificence and biodiversity, ecotourism creates income for neighborhood networks, boosting the protection of environments for future the travel industry.

Coordinated Land-Use Arranging:

Coordinated land-use arranging includes orchestrating preservation needs with metropolitan and country improvement plans. This approach thinks about the biological worth of various regions, assigning zones for preservation, agribusiness, and urbanization to offset human requirements with ecological security.

4. **Contextual analyses in Adjusting Protection and Human Necessities**

Future Outlook: Building Climate-Resilient Ecosystems

Yaguas Public Park epitomizes a cooperative exertion between the Peruvian government, native networks, and protection associations. The recreation area's assignment adjusts the assurance of biodiverse rainforests with the freedoms of native networks to reasonably utilize normal assets.

Gorongosa Public Park, Mozambique:

The reclamation of Gorongosa Public Park in Mozambique includes an all encompassing methodology that joins natural life preservation with local area improvement. The recreation area's administration connects with nearby networks in ecotourism, feasible farming, and schooling, exhibiting the combination of protection and human prosperity.

Chyulu Slopes Preservation and Occupation Program, Kenya:

The Chyulu Slopes Protection and Business Program coordinates preservation with local area improvement in Kenya. By advancing manageable land-use works on, giving elective occupations, and supporting nearby instruction, the program shows a fair methodology that addresses human issues while protecting biodiversity.

5. **Difficulties and Contemplations in Adjusting Preservation and Human Necessities**

Transient Monetary Tensions:

The prompt financial requirements of networks might focus on asset extraction over protection. Adjusting these momentary monetary tensions with long haul maintainability requires carrying out measures that show the financial advantages of protection.

Populace Development and Urbanization:

Populace development and urbanization add to expanded requests for land and assets. Offsetting protection with human requirements includes addressing populace elements and executing shrewd metropolitan intending to limit ecological effect.

Environmental Change Effects:

Environmental change represents extra difficulties to the fragile harmony among preservation and human requirements. The changing environment influences the two biological systems and human networks, requiring versatile procedures that think about the interconnectedness of natural and cultural prosperity.

Worldwide Monetary Imbalance:

Worldwide monetary imbalance impacts the capacity of nations and networks to offset preservation with human necessities. Agricultural countries might confront more noteworthy strain to focus on prompt financial increases over long haul preservation goals, requiring worldwide coordinated effort and backing.

6. **Strategy Structures and Worldwide Coordinated effort**

   Integrating Protection into Improvement Approaches:

   State run administrations can advance manageable concurrence by incorporating preservation needs into public improvement approaches. Integrating protection contemplations into financial improvement plans guarantees that ecological safeguarding is a critical part of more extensive cultural objectives.

   Peaceful accords and Conventions:

   Peaceful accords, like the Show on Organic Variety (CBD), give a structure to worldwide joint effort in biodiversity preservation. Sanctioning and sticking to these arrangements shows a guarantee to offsetting preservation with human requirements on a worldwide scale.

   Economical Advancement Objectives (SDGs):

   The Unified Countries Economical Improvement Objectives

(SDGs) give a thorough structure to offsetting preservation with human necessities. SDG 15, explicitly, centers around life ashore and intends to guarantee the manageable utilization of earthly environments.

7. **The Job of Instruction and Mindfulness**

Natural Instruction:

Natural training is a vital device in encouraging a comprehension of the fragile harmony among preservation and human requirements. By advancing familiarity with biodiversity, biological system administrations, and reasonable practices, schooling assumes a significant part in shaping ecologically cognizant social orders.

Correspondence and Effort:

Successful correspondence and effort endeavors overcome any barrier between preservation associations, policymakers, and nearby networks. Straightforward correspondence fabricates trust, encourages cooperation, and guarantees that preservation drives line up with the desires and needs of networks.

8. **Future Possibilities: Toward Supportable Concurrence**

Future Outlook: Building Climate-Resilient Ecosystems

Mechanical developments, like remote detecting, computerized reasoning, and information investigation, upgrade our capacity to screen and oversee biological systems. These progressions can illuminate more exact and compelling protection systems that think about both environmental and human aspects.

Combination of Nature-Based Arrangements:

Nature-based arrangements include tackling the force of environments to address cultural difficulties. Incorporating these arrangements into metropolitan preparation, agribusiness, and framework improvement adjusts human requirements to the reclamation and preservation of indigenous habitats.

Enabling Nearby People group:

Enabling nearby networks to effectively take part in dynamic cycles and protection drives fortifies the underpinning of maintainable concurrence. Local area commitment guarantees that protection endeavors regard neighborhood points of view and add to local area prosperity.

Chapter 8

Future Outlook: Building Climate-Resilient Ecosystems

The fate of our planet is unpredictably attached to the versatility of its environments despite environmental change. As the effects of a warming environment become progressively clear, the basic to construct environment strong biological systems has never been more critical. This investigation dives into the difficulties presented by environmental change, the systems and developments pointed toward upgrading environment strength, and the cooperative endeavors expected to tie down a maintainable future for a long time into the future.

1. **The Environmental Change Challenge**
   Changing Environment Examples:
   The World's environment is going through huge changes, with climbing temperatures, modified precipitation designs, and an expansion in the recurrence and power of outrageous climate occasions. These progressions present existential dangers to environments and the bunch species that rely upon them.
   Influences on Biodiversity:
   Environmental change disturbs the fragile equilibrium of

biological systems, prompting shifts in species circulations, adjusted movement examples, and changes in the planning of natural occasions. These effects, joined with territory misfortune and debasement, add to the worldwide decay of biodiversity.

Rising Ocean Levels and Sea Fermentation:

The liquefying of polar ice covers and ice sheets adds to rising ocean levels, representing an immediate danger to beach front environments. Moreover, the ingestion of abundance carbon dioxide by the world's seas prompts sea fermentation, further imperiling marine life.

Outrageous Climate Occasions:

The expansion in the recurrence and power of outrageous climate occasions, including storms, dry spells, floods, and rapidly spreading fires, has broad ramifications for biological systems. These occasions can prompt living space annihilation, loss of biodiversity, and disturbances in environment administrations.

2. **Methodologies for Building Environment Versatile Biological systems**

Biological system Based Variation (EbA):

Biological system based variation includes utilizing the administrations given by solid environments to assist networks with adjusting to the effects of environmental change. This approach accentuates the preservation and rebuilding of regular natural surroundings, like backwoods and wetlands, to improve versatility.

Rebuilding and Reforestation:

The rebuilding of debased biological systems and enormous scope reforestation endeavors assume an essential part in building environment versatility. Trees sequester carbon, diminish the gamble of fierce blazes, and add to biodiversity protection, making them fundamental in alleviating and adjusting to environmental change.

Green Foundation Advancement:

Green foundation, including parks, green rooftops, and metropolitan woods, adds to environment versatility in metropolitan regions. These highlights assist with engrossing abundance precipitation, diminish the metropolitan intensity island impact, and give essential environment administrations to nearby networks.

Protection of Biodiversity Areas of interest:

Focusing on the preservation of biodiversity areas of interest — locales with elevated degrees of endemic species — safeguards exceptional environments that are especially defenseless against environmental change. Protecting these regions upgrades in general biodiversity and environment strength.

Environment Savvy Horticulture:

Environment savvy horticultural practices center around maintainable and versatile cultivating techniques. Methods, for example, agroforestry, crop expansion, and accuracy cultivating assist agribusiness with adjusting to changing environment conditions while limiting ecological effect.

Marine Safeguarded Regions and Coral Reef Rebuilding:

Making marine safeguarded regions and executing coral reef rebuilding projects are fundamental for protecting marine environments. These drives relieve the effects of increasing ocean temperatures, sea fermentation, and overfishing on coral reefs and marine biodiversity.

3. **Creative Advances for Environment Strength**

Remote Detecting and Earth Perception:

Remote detecting advancements give significant information to checking and overseeing biological systems. Earth perception satellites can follow changes in land cover, evaluate the soundness of backwoods, and screen the effects of environmental change on a worldwide scale.

Environment Versatile Yield Assortments:

Creating and advancing environment versatile yield assortments is fundamental for food security despite changing environment conditions. These assortments are reared to endure intensity, dry spell, and other environment related burdens, guaranteeing more steady farming yields.

Accuracy Horticulture and Advanced Cultivating:

Accuracy horticulture utilizes innovation like GPS, sensors, and information examination to improve cultivating rehearses. Computerized cultivating stages empower ranchers to go with informed choices, further develop asset proficiency, and adjust to changing environment conditions.

Man-made brainpower (artificial intelligence) for Preservation:

Simulated intelligence applications, including AI calculations, improve protection endeavors by dissecting enormous datasets and distinguishing designs. Simulated intelligence can be utilized to screen natural life, evaluate environment wellbeing, and foresee the effects of environmental change on biological systems.

Quality Altering for Environment Tough Species:

Propels in quality altering advancements offer the chance of establishing environment tough species. While disputable, these advancements could be utilized to upgrade the versatile limits of specific plants and creatures confronting annihilation because of environmental change.

4. **Challenges in Building Environment Versatile Biological systems**

Restricted Subsidizing and Assets:

Sufficient financing is fundamental for carrying out environment versatility procedures. Restricted monetary assets and contending needs present huge difficulties, especially for emerging countries with weak environments.

Worldwide Imbalance and Transformation Abberations:

Worldwide imbalances compound the difficulties of building environment strength. Weak people group in low-pay nations frequently come up short on assets and framework expected to adjust to environmental change influences, prompting differences in strength.

Absence of Political Will and Worldwide Participation:

Building environment versatile biological systems requires solid political will and global participation. The absence of a brought together worldwide way to deal with environmental change impedes the execution of powerful procedures and arrangements.

Unconventionality of Environmental Change Effects:

The capricious idea of environmental change influences makes it trying to foster exact and designated flexibility methodologies. The changeability in territorial and nearby impacts requires versatile administration moves toward that can acclimate to evolving conditions.

5. **The Job of Networks in Environment Versatility**

Local area Based Transformation Systems:

Drawing in neighborhood networks in the turn of events and execution of environment transformation methodologies is vital. Local area based approaches guarantee that drives are socially delicate, address nearby needs, and expand on customary information.

Native Information and Practices:

Native people group frequently have significant information and practices that improve biological system strength. Incorporating native points of view into protection and transformation endeavors advances supportable conjunction with the climate.

Engaging Nearby Navigation:

Engaging nearby networks to partake in dynamic cycles connected with land use and normal asset the executives encourages a feeling of pride and obligation. Comprehensive administration models upgrade the progress of environment strength drives.

6. **Strategy Structures and Global Cooperation**

Mix of Environment Strength into Arrangements:

State run administrations need to coordinate environment

versatility into public arrangements across areas. This incorporates integrating environment contemplations into land-use arranging, horticulture strategies, and metropolitan improvement plans.

Peaceful accords and Responsibilities:

Peaceful accords, like the Paris Understanding, give a structure to worldwide joint effort on environment activity. Nations need to satisfy their responsibilities and work all in all to address the main drivers of environmental change and improve versatility.

Monetary Help for Environment Versatility:

Created countries should satisfy their vows to offer monetary help to agricultural nations for environment versatility drives. This help is significant for carrying out transformation procedures in areas generally powerless against environmental change.

Examination and Information Sharing:

Joint effort in logical exploration and the sharing of information are fundamental for understanding the effects of environmental change and creating powerful versatility systems. Open admittance to data cultivates a worldwide local area of specialists and professionals pursuing shared objectives.

7. **Schooling and Public Mindfulness**

Environment Proficiency:

Environment proficiency drives are imperative for bringing issues to light about the effects of environmental change and the significance of building flexibility. Schooling programs at all levels assist with making a proficient and informed public that can add to environment activity.

Local area Effort and Commitment:

Connecting with networks through outreach projects and correspondence crusades constructs support for environment flexibility drives. Public mindfulness cultivates a feeling of shared liability and energizes maintainable practices at the individual and local area levels.

8. **Future Advancements and Open doors**

Nature-Based Arrangements:

Nature-based arrangements include utilizing environments themselves to address environment challenges. This incorporates ventures, for example, rewilding, biological system rebuilding, and feasible land the board that tackle the force of nature for environment versatility.

Roundabout Economy Practices:

Embracing round economy rehearses limits squander and expands asset productivity. Such practices lessen the natural effect of human exercises and add to the general strength of biological systems.

Metropolitan Greening and Manageable Foundation:

Metropolitan greening drives, combined with manageable foundation improvement, upgrade the strength of metropolitan regions. Green rooftops, penetrable asphalts, and metropolitan parks add to environment transformation and work on the personal satisfaction in urban communities.

Worldwide Cooperation for Protection:

Building environment strong biological systems requires a unified worldwide exertion. Cooperative drives including legislatures, non-administrative associations, organizations, and neighborhood networks can use different mastery and assets for viable preservation.

8.1 Emerging Trends in Conservation Science

Preservation science, as a powerful field, constantly adjusts to the developing difficulties of our quickly evolving planet. Arising patterns in protection science mirror a pledge to imaginative methodologies, state of the art innovations, and interdisciplinary joint effort. This investigation digs into the boondocks of protection science, looking at key patterns that are molding the fate of biodiversity conservation.

1. **Coordinating Innovation for Improved Checking**
   Remote Detecting and Earth Perception:
   Remote detecting advances, including satellite symbolism and automated elevated vehicles (UAVs), reform the observing of biological systems. These devices give high-goal information,

empowering researchers to follow changes in land cover, deforestation, and living space misfortune on a worldwide scale.

Camera Traps and Sensor Organizations:
Camera traps and sensor networks are progressively used to screen untamed life populaces and conduct. These gadgets offer a non-nosy method for social event information on subtle species, contributing significant bits of knowledge into environmental elements and supporting protection endeavors.

Man-made consciousness (artificial intelligence) and AI:
Computer based intelligence and AI calculations break down tremendous datasets, giving more productive and precise evaluations of biodiversity. These innovations can recognize species, foresee environment changes, and advance protection techniques in view of complicated examples and connections.

Ecological DNA (eDNA) Examination:
Ecological DNA examination includes extricating hereditary material from air, water, or soil to identify the presence of species. This harmless method permits specialists to overview biodiversity in oceanic and earthbound environments with more noteworthy awareness.

2. **Versatile Administration and Preservation Arranging**
Dynamic Protection Arranging:
Protection arranging is advancing towards dynamic and versatile methodologies that think about the always changing nature of environments. Coordinating continuous information and criticism circles considers light-footed navigation, guaranteeing that preservation procedures stay successful despite vulnerabilities.

Environment Responsive Preservation:
Protection science is progressively centered around environment responsive systems. Adjusting to the effects of environmental change requires dynamic protection designs that consider moving territories, modified relocation designs, and changing natural

elements.

Preservation in Human-Ruled Scenes:

Perceiving the impact of human exercises on scenes, preservation science is embracing approaches that integrate human-overwhelmed regions. Metropolitan preservation, maintainable land use arranging, and green framework advancement are becoming essential parts of protection systems.

3. **Hereditary qualities and Genomics for Protection**

Hereditary Salvage and Helped Relocation:

Hereditary salvage includes bringing hereditary variety into little or separated populaces to upgrade their flexibility. Helped relocation investigates the movement of species to new living spaces to assist them with adapting to changing ecological circumstances, both worked with by progressions in genomics.

Cryopreservation of Hereditary Material:

Cryopreservation methods empower the drawn out stockpiling of hereditary material, including seeds, incipient organisms, and tissues. This approach fills in as a type of hereditary protection, safeguarding biodiversity and offering an asset for future preservation and reclamation endeavors.

Genomic Ways to deal with Figuring out Variation:

Genomic research gives experiences into the versatile capability of species confronting ecological difficulties. Understanding the hereditary premise of transformation distinguishes populaces with higher flexibility, directing designated preservation endeavors.

4. **Rebuilding Biology and Rewilding**

Enormous Scope Environment Rebuilding:

Rebuilding environment is advancing towards huge scope extends that expect to reestablish whole biological systems. These drives center around once again introducing local species, eliminating obtrusive species, and reestablishing normal cycles to take corrupted scenes back to biological wellbeing.

Rewilding as a Protection System:

Rewilding includes reestablishing normal cycles and permitting biological systems to recapture their environmental intricacy. It frequently incorporates the renewed introduction of cornerstone species to catalyze biological system recuperation and advance biodiversity.

Marine Environment Reclamation:

Reclamation endeavors are growing to marine biological systems, including coral reefs and seagrass beds. Strategies, for example, coral cultivating and living space reclamation plan to restore debased marine conditions and improve the versatility of seaside biological systems.

5. **Protection Money and Inventive Subsidizing Models**

Influence Venture and Protection Money:

Influence speculation channels private capital into preservation projects with the double point of monetary returns and positive ecological results. Protection finance investigates imaginative subsidizing models that influence market-based systems to help biodiversity safeguarding.

Biodiversity Balancing and Pay:

Biodiversity balancing includes making up for the natural effects of advancement projects by putting resources into protection somewhere else. This approach tries to accomplish a net positive effect on biodiversity, adjusting monetary exercises to protection objectives.

Installment for Biological system Administrations (PES):

Installment for Biological system Administrations is acquiring unmistakable quality as a component to monetarily reward networks and landowners for keeping up with sound environments. PES cultivates supportable land the executives rehearses and boosts the preservation of indispensable environment administrations.

6. **Local area Commitment and Resident Science**

Local area Based Preservation Drives:

Preservation science is progressively perceiving the significance of connecting with neighborhood networks in protection endeavors. Local area based drives engage individuals to effectively take part in biodiversity observing, environment reclamation, and maintainable asset the executives.

Resident Science and Information Assortment:

Resident science includes the dynamic contribution of the general population in logical examination and information assortment. Portable applications, online stages, and local area driven projects empower residents to contribute important information, growing the range and size of protection checking.

Native Information and Practices:

Coordinating native information and practices into preservation techniques improves the comprehension of environments. Native people group frequently have important bits of knowledge into supportable asset the executives and add to the social and natural wealth of scenes.

7. **Strategy Systems and Global Joint effort**

Worldwide Protection Arrangements:

Peaceful accords and systems, like the Show on Natural Variety (CBD) and the Worldwide Biodiversity Structure, give an establishment to worldwide joint effort in preservation. These arrangements set targets, rules, and shared responsibilities to address biodiversity misfortune.

Transboundary Protection Drives:

Protection science is advancing transboundary drives that rise above international limits. Cooperative tasks between adjoining nations improve biodiversity insurance, particularly for transient species and environments that range borders.

Comprehensive Direction and Native Freedoms:

Strategies underlining comprehensive dynamic cycles and perceiving the privileges of native people groups add to more successful and fair protection results. This approach guarantees that different points of view are viewed as in preservation arranging and execution.

8. **Moral Contemplations in Preservation Science**

Moral Elements of Hereditary Innovations:

The utilization of hereditary advances in preservation brings up moral issues about mediation in regular cycles. Researchers and policymakers are effectively addressing moral contemplations connected with hereditary alteration, movements, and helped relocation.

Social Value in Preservation:

Preservation science is progressively recognizing the significance of social value in protection drives. Guaranteeing that preservation benefits are dispersed reasonably among networks assists work with trusting, upgrade cooperation, and advance supportable results.

Evenhanded Admittance to Advantages from Preservation Money:

Moral contemplations reach out to the dissemination of advantages from preservation finance drives. Approaches and arrangements need to guarantee that neighborhood networks, particularly those generally underestimated, have fair admittance to the monetary advantages got from preservation exercises.

9. **The Job of Schooling and Public Mindfulness**

Natural Schooling for Feasible Practices:

Natural schooling programs assume a pivotal part in building mindfulness and comprehension of protection issues. Instructing the public cultivates a feeling of obligation, empowering feasible practices and backing for preservation endeavors.

Correspondence and Effort Techniques:

Viable correspondence and effort methodologies overcome any barrier between researchers, policymakers, and general society. Straightforward correspondence fabricates public help, demystifies logical cycles, and underlines the significance of biodiversity preservation.

8.2 Global Collaboration for Ecosystem Resilience

Environment strength, even with environmental change and biodiversity misfortune, requires composed worldwide endeavors. As natural difficulties rise above public lines, the requirement for global coordinated effort has become progressively obvious. This investigation dives into the significance of worldwide joint effort for environment flexibility, looking at the structures, drives, difficulties, and open doors that characterize the aggregate quest for an economical and tough future for our planet.

1. **The Basic for Worldwide Coordinated effort**
   Interconnectedness of Environments:
   Environments work as interconnected frameworks, and aggravations in a single district can have flowing impacts worldwide. Environmental change, contamination, and living space annihilation are transboundary issues that require cooperative answers for address their expansive effects.

   Biodiversity Protection as a Common Obligation:
   Biodiversity, a foundation of biological system strength, knows no international limits. The deficiency of biodiversity in one area of the planet can influence the steadiness and working of biological systems somewhere else. Worldwide coordinated effort is fundamental for address the common obligation of saving Earth's natural variety.

   Environmental Change as a Worldwide Test:
   Environmental change represents a worldwide test that requests aggregate activity. The effects of increasing temperatures, outrageous climate occasions, and ocean level ascent influence countries across mainlands. Relieving and adjusting to environmental change require bound together

endeavors to decrease ozone harming substance outflows and construct environment versatile biological systems.

2. **Structures for Worldwide Cooperation**

   Show on Organic Variety (CBD):

   The CBD is a key worldwide deal that tends to the protection of biodiversity, manageable utilization of its parts, and the fair and evenhanded sharing of advantages. It gives a structure to countries to set targets, trade information, and team up on biodiversity protection methodologies.

   Paris Settlement on Environmental Change:

   The Paris Understanding expects to restrict an Earth-wide temperature boost to well under 2 degrees Celsius above pre-modern levels. It stresses the significance of worldwide coordinated effort in lessening ozone depleting substance emanations and improving the flexibility of biological systems to environmental change influences.

   Economical Improvement Objectives (SDGs):

   The Unified Countries Reasonable Improvement Objectives, especially Objective 15 (Life Ashore), feature the worldwide obligation to safeguarding, reestablishing, and advancing feasible utilization of earthly environments. Accomplishing these objectives requires worldwide participation to address the main drivers of natural corruption.

3. **Transboundary Preservation Drives**

   Preservation Passages and Transboundary Safeguarded Regions:

   Preservation passages and transboundary safeguarded regions advance the availability of biological systems across borders. These drives perceive the requirement for composed protection endeavors to empower the development of species, save biodiversity, and improve biological system flexibility.

   Transient Species Preservation:

Numerous species embrace broad movements that length various nations. Cooperative endeavors, like the Show on the Preservation of Transitory Types of Wild Creatures (CMS), intend to safeguard transient species and their territories, perceiving the significance of global collaboration.

Global Waters Administration:

The strength of marine biological systems is imperative to worldwide flexibility. Peaceful accords, similar to the Unified Countries Show on the Law of the Ocean (UNCLOS), give a structure to the supportable use and preservation of marine assets, underscoring the significance of cross-line coordinated effort.

4. **Challenges in Worldwide Cooperation**

Dissimilar Public Interests:

Disparate public interests and needs can impede worldwide coordinated effort. Contending monetary plans, varying degrees of advancement, and clashing political needs might present difficulties to adjusting countries on shared natural objectives.

Asset Inconsistencies:

Variations in monetary and mechanical assets among countries can hinder powerful coordinated effort. Agricultural nations, frequently more helpless against ecological difficulties, may miss the mark on ability to carry out strong preservation measures without global help.

Political Will and Responsibility:

The outcome of worldwide joint effort relies upon the political will and responsibility of countries. Moving political scenes, changes in administration, and shifting degrees of commitment can affect the coherence and viability of global natural arrangements.

Requirement and Consistence:

Guaranteeing consistence with peaceful accords presents

difficulties. The shortfall of compelling requirement systems and ramifications for rebelliousness might sabotage the execution of settled upon preservation measures.

5. **Open doors for Reinforcing Worldwide Joint effort Comprehensive Dynamic Cycles:**

Comprehensive dynamic cycles that include different partners, including native networks and neighborhood populaces, upgrade the authenticity and adequacy of worldwide coordinated effort. Perceiving the viewpoints and privileges of all partners cultivates a feeling of shared possession in preservation endeavors.

Innovation for Information Sharing and Checking:

Progresses in innovation work with information sharing, checking, and covering natural circumstances. Open-access stages, satellite symbolism, and remote detecting advances empower ongoing data trade, supporting cooperative preservation endeavors.

Limit Building and Information Move:

Limit building programs that enable countries with the information and abilities for compelling preservation are urgent. Cooperative drives that work with the exchange of ability and innovation add to building the strength of biological systems around the world.

Public Mindfulness and Promotion:

Encouraging public mindfulness and promotion for worldwide coordinated effort in protection is imperative. Drawing in residents, common society, and non-legislative associations makes a groundswell of help that can impact policymakers and build up the significance of worldwide collaboration.

6. **Contextual analyses in Fruitful Worldwide Joint effort Amazon Collaboration Deal Association (ACTO):**

ACTO, containing eight Amazonian nations, works together on feasible turn of events and preservation in the Amazon Bowl. The association tends to deforestation, biodiversity misfortune, and environmental change through joint drives, showing the viability of local coordinated effort.

African Parks Organization:

The African Parks Organization is a non-benefit association that teams up with African legislatures to oversee and reestablish safeguarded regions. Through worldwide associations and confidential area commitment, the organization upgrades the preservation of biodiversity and advances maintainable turn of events.

Antarctic Arrangement Framework:

The Antarctic Settlement Framework, endorsed by various countries, assigns Antarctica as a logical safeguard. This cooperative exertion forbids military action, advances logical examination, and saves regional cases, showing fruitful worldwide collaboration in safeguarding a novel and delicate biological system.

7. **The Job of Non-State Entertainers**

Non-Administrative Associations (NGOs):

NGOs assume a significant part in spanning holes and working with coordinated effort between legislatures, networks, and worldwide associations. Their backing, research, and on-the-ground drives add to the outcome of worldwide preservation endeavors.

Confidential Area Commitment:

The confidential area can add to worldwide cooperation through manageable strategic policies, corporate obligation, and interests in protection projects. Public-private organizations influence assets and skill for significant natural drives.

Scholarly and Exploration Establishments:

Scholarly and investigate foundations contribute significant information and advancement to worldwide joint effort. Cooperative examination projects, scholastic trades, and the spread of logical discoveries upgrade the comprehension of biological systems and illuminate protection techniques.

8. Future Possibilities and Arising Models

Worldwide Protection Stages:

Arising models, for example, worldwide protection stages, plan to make comprehensive spaces for countries, associations, and networks to team up. These stages work with discourse, asset sharing, and joint drives to address squeezing natural difficulties.

Green Tact and Eco-Representatives:

The ascent of green tact stresses ecological contemplations in conciliatory relations. Eco-representatives, addressing countries with an emphasis on maintainability, advocate for worldwide cooperation on protection issues and advance harmless to the ecosystem strategies.

Blockchain Innovation for Straightforwardness:

Blockchain innovation, with its straightforwardness and recognizability highlights, holds guarantee for upgrading responsibility in worldwide protection arrangements. Brilliant agreements and decentralized frameworks can guarantee that responsibilities are respected, cultivating trust among teaming up countries.

8.3 The Role of Education and Advocacy

The job of training and support is fundamental in cultivating a worldwide comprehension of ecological difficulties and moving aggregate activity. Schooling furnishes people with the information to see the value in the significance of biological system strength and biodiversity protection. Promotion enhances these standards, activating networks, policymakers, and organizations to participate in reasonable practices and backing global coordinated effort. Together, training and support structure a strong cooperative energy, driving mindfulness, molding mentalities, and catalyzing the extraordinary activities expected to protect our planet for current and people in the future.

Chapter 9

Conclusion

In the immense scene of human getting it, the excursion through different subjects, points of view, and thoughts has been an advancing encounter. As we explore the unpredictable snare of information, it becomes clear that the quest for intelligence is a deep rooted try that consistently develops, adjusts, and shapes our impression of the world. In this far reaching investigation, we have dove into different domains, from the sciences to human expression, from reasoning to innovation, and from history to what's in store. As we finish up this far reaching talk, it is critical to consider the key experiences acquired, the difficulties experienced, and the ramifications for what's in store.

Reflections on the Interconnectedness of Information

One all-encompassing topic that has arisen all through this investigation is the interconnectedness of information. The limits between disciplines are not unbending walls but rather porous layers, permitting thoughts to stream consistently starting with one space then onto the next. For example, the crossing points among science and reasoning have become progressively evident. The logical technique, grounded in exact perception and trial and error, shares shared view with philosophical request, particularly while examining inquiries concerning the idea of the real world, cognizance, and the restrictions of human getting it.

Essentially, innovation, when thought about a particular field, is presently unpredictably woven into the texture of virtually every part of human existence. The harmonious connection between innovative headways and cultural advancement has ended up being certain. From medical care to correspondence, from training to amusement, innovation has changed the manner in which we live as well as tested customary ideas of morals, protection, and the overall influence.

This interconnectedness highlights the significance of taking on an all encompassing way to deal with instruction and critical thinking. A siloed comprehension of individual subjects is at this point not adequate in our current reality where difficulties are mind boggling, diverse, and frequently rise above disciplinary limits. As we push ahead, the capacity to explore the convergences of different fields and orchestrate assorted viewpoints will be a significant expertise in tending to the many-sided difficulties of the 21st 100 years.

Difficulties and Discussions: Exploring the Hazy situations

The quest for information isn't without its difficulties and discussions. Over the entire course of time, the conflict of thoughts has been both the impetus for progress and the wellspring of contention. From the Copernican transformation provoking the geocentric model to contemporary discussions about man-made consciousness and bioethics, scholarly talk has frequently been set apart by pressure and protection from change.

Debates emerge while existing standards are addressed, and groundbreaking thoughts challenge laid out standards. Notwithstanding, it is inside these contentions that the cauldron of development works. The conflict of viewpoints powers a reconsideration of suspicions, prompting the refinement and development of our aggregate comprehension. The cycle might be awkward, however it is a demonstration of the dynamism inborn chasing information.

However, debates likewise feature the requirement for a nuanced and compassionate way to deal with scholarly talk. As we draw in with varying perspectives, basic to cultivate a climate empowers open exchange, decisive reasoning, and a veritable readiness to figure out substitute points of view. Thusly, we add to the progression of information as well as develop a general public fit for exploring intricacies without surrendering to the troublesome entanglements that discussion can bring.

The Basic of Moral Contemplations

In the journey for information, moral contemplations pose a potential threat. The power that accompanies getting it, whether it be mechanical ability or logical revelation, conveys a significant obligation. As we open the secrets of the universe and outfit the capacities to control the essential structure blocks of life, moral systems become irreplaceable.

The progression of man-made consciousness gives a relevant model. The capacity to make machines with mental capacities brings up significant issues about independence, responsibility, and the possible outcomes of releasing such advancements into society. Finding some kind of harmony among development and moral limitation is certainly not a clear errand, and it requires a purposeful exertion from scientists, policymakers, and people in general.

Also, the verifiable stuff of logical and mechanical headways helps us to remember the moral slips by that have went with progress. From the improvement of nuclear weapons to natural corruption, the potentially negative side-effects of unrestrained logical pursuits have made permanent imprints on our shared perspective. The objective, in this way, isn't simply to propel information for the good of its own yet to do as such with a sharp consciousness of the moral ramifications, guaranteeing that progress lines up with the prosperity of humankind and the planet.

The Elements of Long lasting Learning

As we close this investigation, it becomes obvious that the excursion of information is a constant cycle — a powerful odyssey that rises above the limits of formal instruction. Long lasting learning isn't simply an expression however a sober minded way to deal with remaining significant in a world described by fast change. The timeframe of realistic usability of abilities is decreasing, and flexibility has turned into a critical determinant of progress in the expert scene.

In the time of data overflow, developing the capacity to recognize, blend, and apply information has turned into a vital expertise. The conventional model of instruction, with its proper educational plan and characterized span, is giving way to a more adaptable, customized, and progressing growth opportunity. The approach of online stages, open instructive assets, and cooperative learning models has democratized admittance to data, permitting people to fit their learning processes to their particular necessities and interests.

Besides, the convergence of mechanical development and training can possibly alter the manner in which we procure and apply information. Man-made consciousness, increased reality, and virtual learning conditions offer additional opportunities for vivid and intuitive growth opportunities. Be that as it may, the effective joining of these advancements requires smart thought of openness, inclusivity, and the conservation of the human component in the educational experience.

Looking Forward: Exploring the Vulnerabilities

As we look into the future, the scene of information seems both invigorating and overwhelming. The remarkable development of data, combined with the speeding up speed of mechanical development, presents a degree of intricacy that requests our consideration. The difficulties ahead are multi-layered, going from moral situations presented by arising advances to the dire requirement for economical arrangements even with natural emergencies.

The moral ramifications of man-made reasoning, for example, reach out past the bounds of mechanical turn of events. They pervade into issues of civil rights, financial imbalance, and the actual texture of human connections. Finding some kind of harmony between saddling the capability of computer based intelligence and relieving its dangers requires a worldwide discussion and cooperative endeavors to lay out moral systems that defend mankind's inclinations.

Also, the basic to address environmental change and ecological debasement highlights the requirement for interdisciplinary arrangements. The nexus of science, strategy, and public commitment becomes significant in diagramming a course towards supportability. The information acquired from assorted fields should unite to illuminate strategies, innovations, and social changes that can alleviate the effects of environmental change and save the sensitive balance of our planet.

In exploring these vulnerabilities, it is fundamental to encourage a worldwide viewpoint. The difficulties we face are not restricted by lines, and arrangements request global cooperation. The interconnectedness of information reaches out past scholarly disciplines to incorporate a worldwide organization of masterminds, pioneers, and policymakers. Just through aggregate endeavors might we at any point desire to address the mind boggling, interrelated difficulties that characterize our time.

Last Considerations: Embracing the Innate Miracle of Information

As we draw the last strings of this investigation together, it is urgent to recognize the inborn miracle implanted chasing information. From the infinitesimal domains of quantum physical science to the enormous spreads of astronomy, from the perplexing excellence of a scholarly work of art to the harmonies of a melodic organization, the human ability to comprehend and make is spectacular.

As we continued looking for information, we reveal the secrets of presence, wrestle with the significant inquiries that have spellbound masterminds for quite a long time, and add to the continuous embroidery of human accomplishment. The actual demonstration of looking for information is an insistence of our interest, a demonstration of our ability for contemplation, and a festival of the scholarly variety that characterizes our species.

As we pull back from the many-sided trap of thoughts investigated in this talk, it is with a feeling of lowliness, perceiving that the more we learn, the more we understand the endlessness of the unexplored world. The quest for information is definitely not a straight way with a characterized objective; rather, an excursion unfurls in eccentric ways, uncovering new scenes and skylines with each step.

9.1 Summarizing Key Conservation Strategies

Notwithstanding raising ecological difficulties, the basic for compelling protection techniques has become more articulated than any other time. As humankind wrestles with issues, for example, environmental change, biodiversity misfortune, and natural surroundings corruption, an extensive and proactive way to deal with preservation is fundamental. This conversation means to distil and look at key protection systems that address these complex difficulties, underscoring the requirement for a comprehensive and cooperative way to deal with shield the planet's environments.

1. **Biodiversity Protection: Saving the Woven artwork of Life**

   Biodiversity, the rich assortment of life on The planet, is a foundation of biological system wellbeing and strength. Protection endeavors focusing on biodiversity incorporate a scope of systems.

   Safeguarded regions, for example, public parks and untamed life holds, assume an essential part in giving places of refuge to different species. In any case, a powerful methodology stretches out past simple assignment to guarantee these regions are very much made due, enough financed, and associated through natural halls to work with species relocation and hereditary trade.

   Besides, maintainable land the board rehearses are vital in moderating natural surroundings misfortune and fracture. Empowering reasonable ranger service, advancing agroecology, and carrying out dependable metropolitan arranging are vital parts of safeguarding biodiversity. Moreover, people group commitment and strengthening are fundamental; including neighborhood networks in preservation drives cultivates a feeling of stewardship as well as recognizes the natural association between human prosperity and biodiversity.

2. **Environmental Change Alleviation: Exploring the Energy Progress**

Environmental change remains as one of the most squeezing difficulties within recent memory, with broad ramifications for biological systems, networks, and economies. Protection systems to address environmental change center around moderating ozone depleting substance emanations and building flexibility to the progressions currently in progress.

Progressing to environmentally friendly power sources is a key part in environmental change moderation. Putting resources into sun powered, wind, and other economical energy advances is essential to decrease reliance on petroleum products. In addition, advancing energy effectiveness across areas, from transportation to industry, adds to bringing down discharges. Preservation endeavors should likewise underline reforestation and afforestation as trees go about as regular carbon sinks, engrossing and putting away air carbon dioxide.

Variation techniques are similarly urgent, perceiving that some level of environmental change is inescapable. This includes reinforcing the strength of biological systems and networks to endure and recuperate from the effects of an evolving environment. Preservation drives need to focus on the security of environment delicate living spaces, like coral reefs and polar biological systems, while additionally consolidating native information in creating versatile techniques.

3. **Economical Asset The board: Adjusting Human Requirements and Environment Wellbeing**

Preserving regular assets while addressing the necessities of a developing worldwide populace requires a fragile equilibrium. Reasonable asset the board envelops systems that try to fit human exercises with the strength of environments.

In fisheries, carrying out science-based portions, advancing specific and economical fishing rehearses, and laying out marine safeguarded regions are fundamental measures to forestall overexploitation and permit fish populaces to recuperate. Maintainable horticulture rehearses, for example, agroforestry and natural cultivating, focus on soil wellbeing, diminish dependence on synthetic information sources, and advance biodiversity inside farming scenes.

Endeavors to check unlawful logging and natural life dealing are necessary to supportable ranger service. Certificate plans, similar to the Backwoods Stewardship Gathering (FSC), assume a part in guaranteeing that wood and paper items come from capably oversaw timberlands. Also, battling poaching and the unlawful untamed life exchange requests global coordinated effort, severe policing, local area association to address the main drivers of these exercises.

4. **Preservation through Rebuilding: Restoring Debased Biological systems**

Perceiving that numerous environments have proactively been essentially modified or corrupted, reclamation has arisen as a basic protection system. Biological reclamation includes the intentional course of helping the recuperation of environments that have been upset, harmed, or obliterated.

Reforestation endeavors expect to replant trees in deforested or corrupted regions, improving biodiversity, reestablishing soil wellbeing, and relieving environmental change. Wetland reclamation adds to water filtration, flood control, and territory restoration. Marine territory reclamation, including coral reef recovery, tries to turn around the downfall of basic sea biological systems.

Local area inclusion is vital to effective rebuilding drives. Connecting with nearby networks in arranging, executing, and observing reclamation projects guarantees the social responsiveness of mediations as well as cultivates a feeling of responsibility and stewardship.

5. **Natural Schooling and Promotion: Supporting a Protection Ethic**

Advancing ecological training and backing is major to building a worldwide local area that perceives the worth of protection. Instruction fills in as an impetus for conduct change, encouraging a protection ethic that reaches out from people to networks and countries.

Educational program mix, from grade schools to colleges, acquaints understudies with natural standards, ecological morals, and the interconnectedness of environments. Involved encounters, for example, field outings and resident science projects, develop understanding and support a feeling of obligation towards nature.

Public mindfulness missions and promotion endeavors assume a urgent part in preparing networks and impacting strategy.

Protection associations, frequently at the very front of such missions, influence different media stages to impart the desperation of natural issues, advocate for strategy changes, and prepare support for preservation drives.

6. **Coordinating Native Information: Respecting Hundreds of years of Insight**

Native people group all over the planet have supported agreeable associations with their surroundings for a really long time, storing up an abundance of conventional biological information. Perceiving the worth of this astuteness is necessary to powerful preservation procedures.

Native information adds to the comprehension of neighborhood biological systems, species ways of behaving, and environment designs. Integrating conventional practices into protection plans upgrades the adequacy of intercessions as well as regards the freedoms and social legacy of native people groups. Cooperative associations with native networks guarantee that preservation endeavors are logically proper and gainful together.

9.2 Inspiring Action for Ecosystem Preservation

Notwithstanding heightening natural difficulties, the basic for environment protection has become more articulated than any other time. Environments, the complicated trap of daily routine that support all experiencing life forms, are under danger from different human exercises, including deforestation, contamination, environmental change, and territory obliteration. Motivating activity for environment safeguarding requires a complex methodology that draws in people, networks, policymakers, and organizations in a common obligation to stewardship. This talk expects to investigate procedures to light a worldwide ethos of obligation and prod significant activity toward the conservation of Earth's different and delicate environments.

1. **Encouraging Natural Education: The Establishment for Cognizant Activity**

   At the center of moving activity for biological system protection lies the development of ecological proficiency. Grasping the perplexing connections inside environments, fathoming the effect of human exercises on these frameworks, and valuing the interconnectedness of all life shapes the establishment for cognizant and informed activity.

   Instructive establishments assume a significant part in molding natural proficiency. Coordinating natural examinations into school educational plans at all levels gives understudies the information and decisive reasoning abilities expected to understand environmental standards. Past customary study hall settings, experiential learning, for example, nature-based training and field trips, improves the association among people and their current circumstance.

   Additionally, advancing continuous natural instruction for grown-ups is similarly critical. Studios, workshops, and local area outreach projects can engage people with the information expected to pursue informed decisions in their regular routines. By cultivating a more profound comprehension of natural cycles and the ramifications of human activities, ecological education turns into an impetus for proactive commitment to biological system protection.

2. **Developing a Feeling of Spot: Sustaining Nearby Associations**
Motivating activity for biological system safeguarding expects people to feel a significant association with their nearby climate. Developing a feeling of spot includes encouraging a profound appreciation for the special biological systems that encompass us and perceiving the worth they bring to our networks.

Local area based drives, for example, neighborhood ecological clubs, nature strolls, and resident science projects, add to this feeling of spot. At the point when people effectively partake in checking nearby environments, they foster an individual stake in their prosperity. This commitment starts a feeling of obligation and a promise to safeguarding the normal legacy of their district. Besides, advancing feasible practices at the local area level builds up this association. Local area gardens, tree-establishing efforts, and waste decrease projects add to environment wellbeing as well as act as substantial articulations of nearby stewardship. As people observer the positive effect of their aggregate activities, a feeling of satisfaction and possession in the neighborhood climate arises, laying the preparation for more extensive protection endeavors.

3. **Bridling the Force of Innovation: Drawing in a Worldwide Crowd**
In the computerized age, innovation fills in as a useful asset for bringing issues to light and preparing activity on a worldwide scale. Virtual entertainment stages, online missions, and intelligent sites can disperse data, move discourse, and interface people and associations focused on biological system protection.

Computer generated reality and increased reality innovations give vivid encounters that can move people to undermined environments, cultivating an instinctive association and compassion. Live-streaming stages empower constant commitment with natural occasions, making a feeling of worldwide local area joined in the reason for conservation.

Besides, innovation works with resident science drives, empowering people overall to contribute information to environmental examination projects. This democratization of logical cooperation enables individuals to assume a functioning part in checking and grasping biological systems, separating boundaries among researchers and the overall population.

4. **Connecting with Organizations: Molding Economical Practices**

The business area employs critical impact over environments through asset extraction, creation cycles, and inventory network the executives. Moving activity for biological system safeguarding requires a change in perspective in strategic policies toward maintainability, stressing the combination of ecological contemplations into direction.

Corporate obligation goes past lawful consistence to proactively limiting natural effects. Embracing eco-accommodating creation strategies, lessening waste, and putting resources into sustainable power are significant stages. Besides, organizations can effectively add to protection by supporting and funding ecological drives, for example, reforestation projects, untamed life preservation endeavors, and manageable farming projects.

Purchaser interest for reasonable items and moral strategic policies likewise assumes a crucial part. By settling on informed decisions and supporting eco-cognizant organizations, people add to forming market drifts that focus on natural obligation. Thusly, this makes a positive input circle, empowering organizations to adjust their practices to the upsides of a cognizant buyer base.

5. **Strategy Backing: Catalyzing Fundamental Change**
Government arrangements use enormous impact over the administration and protection of biological systems. Supporting for strategies that focus on preservation, reasonable asset the executives, and environment activity is a urgent road for moving fundamental change.

Resident commitment to the arrangement making process is fundamental. People and networks can use their aggregate voice to advocate for regulation that safeguards biological systems, saves biodiversity, and mitigates the effects of environmental change. Grassroots developments, public missions, and joint efforts with natural associations can enhance these backing endeavors.

Global collaboration is similarly imperative, taking into account that numerous natural difficulties rise above public lines. Arrangements and settlements that address issues, for example, deforestation, untamed life dealing, and fossil fuel byproducts require worldwide coordinated effort. People can add to this work by supporting worldwide associations, partaking in worldwide environment strikes, and advancing familiarity with the interconnectedness of biological systems across the planet.

6. **Monetary Valuation of Biological system Administrations: Presenting the Defense for Protection**
Environments give a horde of administrations fundamental for human prosperity, including clean air and water, fertilization of yields, environment guideline, and sporting open doors. Featuring the financial worth of these administrations can be an undeniable case for environment conservation.

Integrating the idea of normal capital into financial structures recognizes the unmistakable advantages that environments give. Appointing financial worth to administrations like wetland filtration, carbon sequestration, and biodiversity preservation highlights the significance of saving unblemished biological systems.

This monetary viewpoint stretches out to ecotourism, which can give monetary motivators to the conservation of normal regions. Reasonable the travel industry rehearses that focus on natural protection, local area commitment, and insignificant environmental effect can produce income for neighborhood economies while safeguarding the very attractions that draw guests.

7. **Social Stories: Meshing Preservation into the Structure holding the system together**

Social stories have the ability to shape cultural qualities and ways of behaving. Moving activity for biological system protection includes meshing preservation into the texture of social stories, making it a common and praised part of human personality.

Craftsmanship, writing, music, and narrating can act as strong vehicles for conveying the magnificence and significance of biological systems. Social celebrations, shows, and exhibitions that celebrate nature cultivate a feeling of veneration and association with the climate.

In native societies, the entwining of otherworldliness and natural stewardship gives a rich embroidery of shrewdness. Perceiving and regarding these social accounts is fundamental, as they frequently offer comprehensive viewpoints on mankind's relationship with the regular world. By integrating different social points of view into the more extensive protection talk, a more comprehensive and successful way to deal with environment safeguarding arises.

9.3 The Ongoing Journey in a Changing Climate

In the unfurling story of human life, the ongoing part is set apart by a significant and extraordinary reality — facing a daily reality such that the environment is changing at an exceptional rate. The continuous excursion in a changing environment isn't simply a logical adventure however a lived insight, influencing biological systems, networks, and the actual texture of our social orders. This excursion requests a complex reaction that includes transformation, relief, and an aggregate obligation to building flexibility.

Variation Notwithstanding Vulnerability

Adjusting to a changing environment is a powerful interaction that includes changing in accordance with new ecological circumstances, developing weather conditions, and the related difficulties that emerge. Networks all over the planet are now wrestling with the effects of an evolving environment, from rising ocean levels and outrageous climate occasions to shifts in precipitation examples and disturbances in farming.

Transformation systems incorporate a range of approaches, going from the improvement of environment strong foundation to the execution of feasible horticultural practices. Waterfront people group are investigating inventive arrangements, for example, ocean walls and mangrove rebuilding to relieve the impacts of rising ocean levels and tempest floods. Ranchers are exploring different avenues regarding dry spell safe yields and water protection procedures to support agrarian efficiency notwithstanding changing precipitation designs.

Significantly, variation is definitely not a one-size-fits-all undertaking. It requires setting explicit arrangements that consider the novel difficulties looked by changed areas, networks, and biological systems. Embracing native information and neighborhood astuteness becomes vital in creating compelling transformation methodologies, perceiving the profound association among networks and their surroundings.

Relief: Graphing a Supportable Way ahead

Relief, then again, centers around tending to the underlying drivers of environmental change by diminishing ozone harming substance outflows. The excursion toward relief includes a central change in the manner social orders produce and consume energy, oversee land use, and move toward modern cycles.

Progressing to sustainable power sources is a key part in moderation endeavors. Moving away from petroleum derivatives to sun powered, wind, hydro, and other practical choices is essential in checking the carbon impression. Nations and enterprises are progressively putting resources into clean energy advancements, perceiving the basic of decoupling monetary development from fossil fuel byproducts.

Economical land the board likewise assumes a vital part in relief. Timberland preservation, reforestation, and forestalling deforestation are fundamental systems to sequester carbon and save biodiversity. Moreover, feasible horticulture rehearses, for example, agroforestry and natural cultivating, add to both moderation and transformation by improving soil wellbeing and lessening dependence on compound sources of info.

Relief isn't exclusively the obligation of legislatures and ventures; it requires individual and aggregate activity. Taking on energy-effective works on, decreasing waste, and pursuing cognizant decisions about utilization add to the more extensive work to moderate environmental change. The excursion towards supportability is a cooperative one, including a range of partners, from policymakers and organizations to networks and people.

Building Strength: An Aggregate Undertaking

Building strength notwithstanding a changing environment is a continuous excursion that requests a comprehensive and coordinated approach. Strength isn't just about returning from shocks and stresses yet additionally about expecting, getting ready for, and gaining from them.

At the local area level, building strength includes creating vigorous social designs, putting resources into instruction and medical care, and making versatile administration frameworks. Engaging nearby networks to effectively take part in dynamic cycles guarantees that versatility techniques are educated by their special necessities and encounters.

Biological system strength is similarly basic. Securing and reestablishing normal natural surroundings, advancing biodiversity, and taking on reasonable asset the executives rehearses add to the capacity of biological systems to endure and recuperate from unsettling influences. Perceiving the interconnectedness of human prosperity and biological system wellbeing is key to building strength on a worldwide scale.

Besides, mechanical developments and data sharing assume a vital part in improving strength. Early admonition frameworks for outrageous climate occasions, environment demonstrating, and information driven direction engage networks to plan for and answer the effects of environmental change successfully.

As the excursion in a changing environment unfurls, the idea of strength reaches out past the natural and social spaces to incorporate financial frameworks. Making economies that are versatile, comprehensive, and manageable adds to in general flexibility. Green innovations, round economies, and socially dependable strategic policies are fundamental parts of a tough financial structure.

The Basic of Worldwide Joint effort

In the continuous excursion in an evolving environment, the difficulties are complicated, interconnected, and worldwide in nature. The basic of coordinated effort on a worldwide scale couldn't possibly be more significant. Environmental change is an aggregate issue that requests aggregate arrangements.

Peaceful accords, like the Paris Understanding, give a system to worldwide coordinated effort on environment activity. In any case, the progress of such arrangements depends on the responsibility and dynamic cooperation of countries, organizations, and networks. Overcoming any barrier among created and agricultural nations, guaranteeing monetary help for weak countries, and working with the exchange of green advances are vital parts of worldwide coordinated effort.

Additionally, recognizing and tending to the civil rights aspects of environmental change is basic to powerful cooperation. Weak people group, frequently least answerable for ozone depleting substance emanations, endure the worst part of environment influences. Hence, environment activity should be grounded in standards of value and equity, perceiving the verifiable obligation of certain countries for the present status of the environment.